LoveSong

EXPLORING GOD, MUSIC AND THE MYSTERY OF TRUE LOVE

DAVID PARKER

ARTWORK BY BEN PARKER

Published by New Generation Publishing in 2021

Copyright © David Parker 2021

First Edition

The author asserts the moral right under the Copyright, Designs and Patents Act 1988 to be identified as the author of this work.

All Rights reserved. No part of this publication may be reproduced, stored in a retrieval system or transmitted, in any form or by any means without the prior consent of the author, nor be otherwise circulated in any form of binding or cover other than that which it is published and without a similar condition being imposed on the subsequent purchaser.

ISBN
    Paperback   978-1-80031-070-4
    Hardback   978-1-80031-069-8
    Ebook   978-1-80369-009-4

www.newgeneration-publishing.com

CONTENTS

PRELUDE: Songs 1 and 2 1
An awakening to Love and the beginning of a journey of discovery.

OVERTURE: Songs 3 - 6 11
A brief look at the history and origin of the love song – the goal of the book, and a Love Song challenge.

THE FIRST MOVEMENT: Songs 7 - 9 25
Jesus to Paul, a look at the importance attributed to Love in the New Testament.

THE SECOND MOVEMENT: Songs 10 - 27 37
An investigation into two types of Love, the hobby of arrow spotting and the power of true Love.

INTERLUDE: Song 28 100
A short reflection.

THE THIRD MOVEMENT: Songs 29 - 34 104
What true Love looks like and how to live a life of Love.

FINALE: Songs 35 - 40 141
The One Universal Love Song and the invitation to sing along.

ENCORE: Appendices 169

PRELUDE

So you crashed the plane and there's hell to pay,
I'm making it plain
I love you anyway
You made a fool out of me today. I'm breaking the rule
I love you anyway'

                         'Love Anyway' by Mike Scott

1. **LOVE IS IN THE AIR** 1977

Have you ever had a life changing moment?

What I mean is, as you look back, has there been a time or a day, a conversation or a decision, an event or an encounter, that has impacted you to such an extent that your life has taken a new direction and changed forever?

It's likely that most of us can identify a few 'crossroads' moments in our lives which have altered things for the better or for the worse. Some may spring to mind instantly. Others may come to our awareness through hindsight or as we spend time reflecting.

For me, two such experiences immediately come to the forefront of my mind. Whilst these occurred over 20 years apart, they are significantly connected. For one thing, both happened in the country of New Zealand.

Another is they both involved 'Love'.

The **first** situation occurred between Christmas and New Year back in 1982. Allow me to set the scene.

The location is the west coast of New Zealand's South Island. I had taken a gap year, and was heading towards Australia with a year-long working visa in my passport. En-route were several planned stopovers, one of which was a month in New Zealand.

On this day, I was driving an old, battered, Fiat car with a broken muffler that had been (kindly?) lent, and I was heading south on a fairly remote stretch of the main highway. In the passenger seat was my old school friend and travelling companion, Stuart.

The sky, which had for some time looked threatening, delivered the first spats of rain to the windscreen. As I peered through the gloom along the straight road ahead, I could see we were approaching a long layby. There were no vehicles parked there, but as I got closer, I saw two figures huddled together, leaning forward with their arms outstretched and their thumbs out.

Hitchhikers were certainly not in short supply on the main routes of New Zealand but due to space restrictions, we had tended to limit our pick-ups to solo travellers. This hopeful pair had plenty of time to get ready for our approach as the noise from the broken muffler would have provided adequate warning, whilst we were still some way off.

As we approached, a quick conversation took place between Stuart and I – do we stop, or do we keep going? We were a bit behind schedule time wise – would this hold us up further? Do we have enough room? Were we in for a full-on storm?

'You're the driver, it's up to you' voiced Stuart as we drew level with the start of the layby. I had a split second to decide. I chose in that moment to keep going: 'It's too late to stop anyway,' I remember thinking as I drove past the two hunched figures.

I am not sure what it was that made me hit the brakes and suddenly pull into the end part of the layby, contrary to the decision I had just made. But as the Fiat came to a stop, the sound of an approving cheer and running feet towards the car were drowned out by a loud backfire. The rear doors opened and in hopped two drenched but grateful females.

We set off again and we were soon sharing our travel stories of where we had been and where we were heading. I looked in the rear-view mirror. I could only see one of the hitchhikers, the one who had introduced herself as Kirsten, but I remember thinking 'What a beautiful face,' and struggling to keep my eyes on the road for the rest of the journey.

Love at first sight?

I am not sure about that, but I often think back to that day and wonder what if I hadn't stopped? What if in that split second moment, I hadn't pulled into that layby? What would my life be like and where would I be right now?

You see that bedraggled hitchhiker with the beautiful face became my wife. We have been married since 1988, which in years is…? Well, you can work it out!

For the **second** life changing event, we need to fast forward to 2003. We are at this point living in New Zealand having moved out there from the UK in 1992. Kirsten and I were both on staff at a local church, and as part of that team, our senior leader every year would encourage us to attend an annual leadership conference together, which always proved to be a valuable time of input, learning and encouragement.

In 2003 however, we were unable to go with the rest of the team. To avoid missing out altogether, we checked out alternative conferences but each one we found was either at the wrong time or in the wrong place. Nothing seemed to fit or work, so as a last resort, we decided to do our own conference.

My parents, who lived in the UK, owned a small holiday home on the edge of our hometown overlooking the lake. They would travel over every year and spend a couple of months there during summer, hence avoiding the UK winter. The rest of the time it was empty, and we were asked to 'keep an eye on it', which meant we could use it whenever we wanted.

Looking back, I wish we had made more use of it, but on this one occasion it became our conference venue. Kirsten and I arrived for a 2-night stay with basic provisions, a portable cassette player and a set of teaching tapes that we knew nothing about.

That tape set changed our lives.

In fact, it turned out to be the most impacting 'conference' we had ever attended, yet there was just the two of us.

The tape set was called 'Unshared Love' by a gentle, wise, fatherly Bible teacher called Bob Mumford.[1] There were 14 sessions on different tapes, each around 30-40 minutes with summary

---

[1] Bob Mumford's ministry is called 'Life changers' based in North Carolina. I'm not sure if this series is still available but the teaching is covered in the book **"The Agape Road: Journey to Intimacy with the Father"** (Destiny Image Publications 2006). Check out this and other resources at www.lifechangers.org

notes and discussion points. The series introduced us to a whole new way of thinking about love in relation to life and faith.

We came away from our intimate 'conference', aware that we were different. There were no fireworks or any form of hyped motivation, just an acknowledged awareness that something had changed at a deep level within us.

2. WE FOUND LOVE 2011

We returned home after our two nights away, aware that we were unable to adequately explain to anyone how our time away had impacted and changed us. In fact, I don't think we even knew. Therefore, we did the best thing we could have done. We said nothing.

Apart from a brief report that we were asked to circulate to the leadership team, we kept quiet. We shared nothing. We sat on it and stored away all we had heard and learnt.

Jesus once told a story about a man who was working as a labourer in a field, and one day as he was digging, he discovered a hoard of buried treasure. When he found it, he immediately buried it again, went and sold everything he had, and then bought the field. [2]

In a strange way, that story connected with just how we were feeling. We had discovered this valuable treasure and the natural desire was to

---

[2] This one verse parable is found in Matthew's gospel chapter 13 verse 44. A parable is a story with a parallel meaning. Jesus is a masterful orator - Who else could tell such a great story in so few words? Topic for Discussion: Should all church sermons be this long?

start sharing it with everything that moved: to shout it from the rooftops.

But we knew that it was not the time. So, we 'hid' it again and went about the process of buying the field. It was necessary we 'owned it' for ourselves.

We began a journey of discovery. We read, studied, and researched the vast theme of love, placing new findings alongside what we had already learnt. Over time we found our understanding expanding as fresh insights came to light. We would share any new thoughts and ideas with each other.

We would spend time discussing the implications this was having on our faith, beliefs and life focus, and wondering where this would take us.

Over two decades later, I now look back and remember those two nights away at the place by the lake on the other side of the world. It is still the most life changing 'conference' that Kirsten and I have ever attended.

Love has since become the foundation of everything for us, with all other things resting on that foundation. We now feel a sense that we have truly 'bought the field' and invested all we have in it.

Yet we are also aware of the unfathomable depths of this Love and there is always this underlying feeling that we have barely scratched the surface.

Nevertheless, it has become our 'Song'.

Some of what we have learnt, we have had the privilege to be able to share both individually and together in churches, seminars, and other forums.

The heart of it is now in this book.

But all we have learnt has been built on that initial revelation from that old tape set by Bob Mumford…so to him is this 'LoveSong' dedicated.

OVERTURE

You threw the blame. What a role to play! My story's the same.
I love you anyway
You dealt the blow and you burst the ball. I'm letting you know,
I love you most of all

Love Anyway' by Mike Scott

3. CRAZY LITTLE THING CALLED LOVE 1979

Love – A simple four-letter word, yet one that has had more stories written, poems recited and songs sung about it than any other subject.

Of those three categories, it is the latter – the songs – that seem to have this ability to influence us in significant ways in a short space of time. This is probably because the unique thing about a 'love song' is that it often combines all categories at once: a lyrical poem that is put to music.

When the power of music connects with the emotion of love, crazy stuff can happen – something potentially explosive, which can affect the human soul in a deep and meaningful way.

[3]

Before reading on, have a go at answering this question. **Do you know what the biggest selling worldwide single is since records began?**

---

[3] Every now and then through this book, you will come across this 'Have a Go' icon, which is an invite for you to partake interactively. This may take the form of a question to answer, something for you to ponder, guess at, read or reflect on.

This one song sold an incredible 33 million copies, and as this was before the era of online downloads, we are talking physical units sold - in other words this was people going into a shop and paying hard earned cash over the counter. (Yes, that really did happen at one time in ancient history.)

The answer is Elton's John's *'Candle in the Wind'* re-released in 1997, a song written originally about Marilyn Monroe, but lyrically changed to become a tribute song following the death of Princess Diana.

On the cover of the single were the words:

"In Loving Memory...".

It was like the song became a vehicle for people around the world to connect in some powerful way, in channelling their feelings for Diana. This seemed to happen in three ways:

Firstly, by connecting with the lyrics of the song.

Secondly, by having a lasting memorial - something physical as a permanent reminder.

Thirdly (and perhaps most significantly), the physical purchasing of the song seemed to be a very real way that individuals could 'express their love' and connect with (and so gain the sense of becoming a part of) something much bigger. It was like an opportunity suddenly existed to become part of a huge global 'choir' expressing a unified outpouring of grief and emotion.

The song became a 'snapshot' love song for the world to sing for that one tragic, never to be forgotten event. [4]

Without doubt, music has this powerful ability to bring people together.

It can happen on a global scale as demonstrated with events such as 'Live Aid' or as already mentioned, Princess Diana's death.

It also happens on a smaller scale, for example whenever people gather for a concert or gig.

One of my favourite pastimes throughout my life has been going to see live concerts.

---

[4] By the way, looking at the list of the top 10 all-time best sellers which have sold upwards of 15 million copies, 3 are songs from popular movies: Namely **'I will Always Love You'** from the Bodyguard, **'Everything I do, I do for you'** from Robin Hood and **'My Heart will go on'** from Titanic. It's interesting that each one is based around the love relationship between the movie's main characters.

I have over the years attended at least 200 gigs from pubs to stadiums, each one holding special memories. I have been privileged to see some of the great artists and bands, and if I ever get together with other people who have a like-minded passion, I can while away hours swapping stories of such occasions.

Looking back, my favourite moments tend to be when iconic songs that everyone knows are sung live.

For me, there is nothing like 100, or 1,000, or 10,000, or 100,000 individual people coming together from all over the place to one venue and becoming one voice together in the singing of a well-known anthem. [5]

You know when you come out of a show and your voice has gone, it's been a good night!

However, it is probably true to say that love songs are not predominantly written for performance in arenas. They tend to be written with a much more intimate setting in mind.

---

[5] When I get into conversations about this, I often get asked what's the best gig I've ever been to? Answer: Queen at Wembley Stadium in 1986 – Freddie Mercury's last tour – released officially on DVD and available for all to experience. The gig was also enhanced by a superb support band line up: Status Quo, The Alarm and INXS.

Most of us can probably relate to the fact that certain songs can evoke powerful memories when we hear them.

For example, maybe one day you are driving in the car, heading to a business meeting. The radio is on but you are not really aware of it as your thoughts are focused on the upcoming agenda.

Suddenly, the radio DJ plays a song that you haven't heard for years, yet as soon as you hear it something happens.

Something connects. Something resonates within you and immediately any thoughts about the morning's meeting have gone.

It is as if you are transported in a time machine back to a particular moment, place, event, or person. You begin to feel and sense things almost as if you were back there.

Many couples have a 'special' song that can be associated with the first time they met, or perhaps a special occasion or a romantic evening. Whenever that song is played, it's as if they are transported back to that former time.

It is when we experience this that we become aware of the strong connection that songs or pieces of music have had, and continue to have on us, at a deep, personal level.

4. SILLY LOVE SONGS 1976

However, it is not all roses and romance.

Within the 'love song' category are those tracks that deal with lost love, separation, divorce and heartbreak and hearing those songs can also stir up memories and emotions of past relationships – painful ones.

Then of course some songs, as good as they are, may not be appropriate for certain occasions.

For example, surely no-one would want to walk down the aisle to Rhianna's *'Unfaithful'*

Or would you want to slow dance to *'If you Leave me Now'* by Chicago at your wedding reception?

How would the brilliant but ever so slightly sinister *'Every Breath you Take'* by the Police go down on a first date?

Or on the grand occasion of a Golden wedding anniversary, I can't see U2's *'I still haven't found what I'm looking for'* going down too well

And I'm sure *'Another one bites the Dust'* by Queen may raise some eyebrows at a funeral…

5. (Birds do it, Bees do it). LET'S DO IT, LET'S FALL IN LOVE 1928

So where did these melodic stories of love begin? What is their origin?

Well, obviously love songs in various guises have been around for centuries, as studies of ancient civilisations and cultures have revealed.

Charles Darwin in the *The Descent of Man'* was of the opinion that the subject of love is the "commonest theme of our songs" [6] and interestingly pointed to the melodic vocalisations of birdsong as the origin of the birth of music. He was especially intrigued by the role birdsong melodies played in the courtship and mating behaviours. [7]

But a significant and possibly controversial explanation of the birth of love songs can be found in Denis de Rougemont's book "*Love in the Western World.*"[8] De Rougemont's suggestion is that the love song grew out of the courtly ballads of the troubadours,

---

[6] *The Descent of Man* by Charles Darwin (1871 John Murray).

[7] 'Love songs - the Hidden History' by Ted Gioia (2015 Oxford University Press) also has fascinating insights into bird song.

[8] 'Love in the Western World' by Denis de Rougemont (New Postscript Edition 1983 Princeton University Press). The book was originally written in 1939.

establishing love alongside romance, side by side with each other. He suggests this began a gradual decline away from the historical 'Christian notion of love'.

Whether this is true or not, it can be argued that in society today, the word 'love' is strongly associated with romance or certainly strong emotional feelings of one to another.

What's more, it is not an uncommon belief expressed today that this thing called love is one of the most important, if not *the* most important of all human needs. You don't have to be of 'Christian' persuasion to hold this viewpoint. Many people of different faiths (or indeed no faith) agree that to love and to be loved is the most vital thing in life.

Significant research has also reached this conclusion.

One of the most elaborate surveys of all time involved the tracking of physical and emotional wellbeing of 2 population groups over a staggering 75-year period.

George Vaillant, a psychiatrist who directed the study for 30 of those 75 years, concluded that there appeared to be two foundational key elements to holistic wellbeing:

"One is love. The other is finding a way of coping with life that does not push love away."[9]

Now if we turn for a moment to the 'Christian notion of love' (using de Rougemont's terminology), the sources of which are the pages of the Bible, we can discover that there is much within them on the subject of Love.

At first glance there seems to be agreement on one important thing: It appears (to me anyway) that the Bible claims that Love is indeed the *most* important thing.

However, this does raise a big question: 'What is meant and understood by 'Love'?

This is where things get interesting.

The Bible goes on to state that God is the *source* of Love and this Love is very different from the world's understanding of what love is.

This implies that what we commonly perceive as love from the world's viewpoint, may in fact not be love at all and that 'True Love' is of a different kind.

In this book, in a very down to earth way, I want to focus on unwrapping the nature of love, investigating

---

[9] This survey is known as the 'Grant and Glueck study' undertaken at Harvard Medical school between 1939 and 2014. The study is actually still ongoing and has since diversified by studying the offspring of the original participants. Check out www.adultdevelopmentstudy.org/grantandglueckstudy

it from the Biblical viewpoint in line with modern-day perceptions of love, with the aim of trying to discover what 'True Love' really is.

At the same time, I want to bring alongside some of those 'courtly love songs' (again using de Rougemont's terminology).

You see, as I have already confessed, I have a soft spot for our 'modern day Troubadours' and let's face it, between them we have a vast catalogue of classic songs that have impacted (and continue to impact) many lives.

However, just before we launch right in with the First Movement, to use a good old Monty Python catchphrase:
'and now for something completely different.' [10]

---

[10] Monty Pythons Flying Circus – BBC TV Comedy Show broadcast 1969-1974. This catchphrase became the title of the Python's first film in 1971.

6. LOVESONG 1989

You may have noticed that there is a bit of a variation on traditional chapters in this book. Did you notice that the six numbered headings, you've read so far are all Song Titles? Did you also notice they each contain the word 'Love'? In other words, they all can claim to be a Love Song'. You may have put two and two together and realised that the numbers after each song title refer to a year - in fact the year that song or a version of the song was officially released.

So, for you lovers of popular music and fans of 'PopMaster'[11] quiz, here is a challenge for you which you can do as you read through the book, should you wish for a light hearted diversion.

As you get to each song/chapter heading write down the name of the artist/ band who performed that song.

---

[11] PopMaster is BBC Radio 2's Music quiz on Ken Bruce's show every weekday morning at 10.30am (as at the time of writing).

There are 40 of them. [After all the BBC official best-selling song charts since the 1950's has always been a Top 40.] The date is a clue because obviously in some cases there are different songs with the same titles.

Recap on the first 6 and when you've finished the book, you'll find all the answers in the back in Appendix C.

Having said all that, let's (properly) begin.

THE FIRST MOVEMENT

I can hear you scream, like a branded slave. It's only a dream
I love you anyway
You've got a war to wage. Chief to obey. Foe to engage
I love you anyway
You hunker down. Feeling small. Judging the clown
I love you most of all

'Love Anyway' by Mike Scott

7. ALL YOU NEED IS LOVE 1967

There's an account in the very first book of the New Testament called Matthew, where an expert in the Jewish law approached Jesus with a question.[12] He asked Jesus what was the most important and greatest commandment of all. Now you may have in your mind that there were 10 commandments, but in fact the Jewish law had 613 commandments. [The 10 commandments were just the first 10].

So, this expert was really asking Jesus what was top of the Commandment charts - what was Number 1 out of 613?

This was His response: *'You shall love the Lord your God with all your heart, with all your soul, and with all your mind.' "This is the first and greatest commandment.'"* NIV [13]

---

[12] Matthew is one of 4 eyewitness accounts of the life of Jesus. They are known as The Gospels (gospel simply means 'Good News'). You can read this encounter in the 22nd Chapter verses 34-40.

[13] NIV stands for 'New International Version', one of many different Bible versions that have been translated into English. I use a variety of versions throughout this book and the list of abbreviations can be found in Appendix B, along with information on why there are so many.

And then He continues giving the expert more than he bargained for...
"And the second is like it: 'you shall love your neighbour as yourself.'" NIV

Fair enough.

But then in verse 40, Jesus says the most astonishing thing:
"'All the Law and the Prophets hang on these two commandments.'" NIV

Now hang on...

Did Jesus just say all the law and all the prophets? Because you see this was a way of referring to the totality of scripture.

The Christian faith traditionally would recognise the totality of scripture as the collection of books that make up the Bible - sometimes referred to as Holy Scripture - and that comprises the Old Testament and the New Testament. But, of course in Jesus' time there was no New Testament - it hadn't been written yet.

So, for Jesus, the totality of written scripture was what we know today as the Old Testament; in simplified terms the first part is the law and the latter part is the prophets.

So, Jesus was in fact saying…the whole of scripture can be summarised as this:

Love God,
Love others.

Full Stop.

Maybe the band who wrote the song in this chapter's heading, really did get it right:

'Love **is** all you need!'

8. LABELLED WITH LOVE 1981

It's impossible for most of us who are not of the Jewish faith, to appreciate the significance of this comment.

The 613 commandments that made up the law were what God gave to Moses on Mount Sinai, as recorded in the Old Testament book of Exodus, starting in Chapter 20 with the 10 Commandments. Each one of the 613 were to be memorised, strictly observed and outworked. They were holy, they were sacred, they were unchangeable, because they were words from God. This was Jewish life - pleasing God by rigidly obeying all the commandments.

And so along comes Jesus and in one brief sentence, he takes those 613 commandments, the entire foundation of Jewish life, screws them up in a ball together, attaches on top a label marked 'Love', and hands it back.

There's one thing you have to say about Jesus - he wasn't short on boldness.

Whilst this, along with most of Jesus's teachings,

went down like a lead balloon with the religious hierarchy, it seems the everyday people were finding his words increasingly compelling. The size of the crowds that started to follow him around was growing all the time.

But it wasn't just the words that drew the people, it was the fact Jesus welcomed them, engaged with them, had time for them, prayed for them, and healed them. For the first time, people were getting a demonstration of love in action.

But did this `Love thing` catch on? What happened after Jesus died?

9. LOVE IS ALL AROUND 1994

One of the leading characters of the New Testament is the Apostle Paul.

When we first encounter him in the book of Acts [14] he is a deeply religious, law abiding Jew who lived meticulously 'by the book', describing himself as "*a Hebrew of Hebrews*"[15] with the confident self-declaration found in Philippians 3:6 that he '*obeyed the law without fault*' NLT.

So zealous was he that he became a leader in the persecution of the growing Jesus movement, determined to wipe it out altogether.

That is until his dramatic Damascus Road conversion as described in Chapter 9, causing a total and radical transformation (including a name change from Saul to Paul).

You've got to smile and admire God's sense of humour.

---

[14] The book of Acts, or Acts of the Apostles, appears in the New Testament after the four Gospels. It was written by Luke and follows on from his gospel. It accounts for the birth of the Church following Jesus' death, resurrection and ascension.

[15] 'Top of the Class' or 'Best of the Best' would be an equivalent terminology we may use.

One of the most radical opposers of the Christian faith ends up overseeing, visiting and caring for various churches, the very ones he was initially trying to destroy!

How ironic is it that in this role, he wrote a number of pastoral letters (or 'epistles' as they were called) which end up as the backbone of the New Testament?

How doubly ironic is it that the inclusion of 13 of these epistles makes him one of the leading contributors to the writings that has established Christianity as the one of the world's leading religions?

According to one internet blog researcher (who has obviously got too much time on their hands, but to whom I am extremely grateful), Paul wrote 50,190 words out of the New Testament's 179,011 total words (based on KJV [16]).

That means Paul wrote about 28% of the New Testament! [17]

---

[16] King James Version - See Appendix B

[17] www.alecsatin.com/how-much-of-the-new-testament-was-written-by-paul - a great article if you love stats.

Now whilst I'm not going to check the validity of the above statistics by counting up, the point is Paul's contribution to the New Testament is hugely significant.

Therefore, his writings should be a good indication as to whether the subject of Love held the same radical importance to the early church as it did for Jesus.

So, what did Paul think and write about Love?

The fact that he did at all proves the dramatic change he went through. But to what extent?

Let's turn to some of these New Testament letters written to the churches that he looked after and oversaw:

To the Corinth Church
An entire chapter within Paul's first letter to the Corinthians is dedicated to love. [18] If you've been to lots of weddings, chances are you will be familiar with it, as it is one of the most common passages chosen for such occasions. It is a stunning chapter but the context is not so much about marriage, it's about a whole way of living.

---

[18] 1 Corinthians 13 – often referred to as the 'Love chapter'

Paul lists a number of activities and states that whatever is done, if it's not done in Love, it's worth nothing. Love should be foundational to everything we do. He then finishes off the chapter –

Faith is important, Hope is important *'...but the **greatest** is **Love**' NKJV.*

We'll return to this chapter later on!

To the Church in Rome

Included in his writings to the Romans, Paul teaches a directive that clearly mirrors Jesus' teaching:

The commandments, "You shall not commit adultery," "You shall not murder," "You shall not steal," "You shall not covet," and whatever other command there may be, are summed up in this one command: "Love your neighbour as yourself." [10] Love does no harm to a neighbour. Therefore, Love is the fulfilment of the Law'. NIV[19]

---

[19] Romans 13:9-10

To the Colossian Church

In the third chapter of this four-chapter letter, Paul lists several attributes that should be evident in the life of a Christian believer including mercy, kindness, humility, gentleness and patience, and then adds…

'But **above all** these things put on **Love**, which binds us all together in perfect harmony' NLT. [20]

[One translation uses the phrase '*highest good*', another '*the perfect thing that binds all other things together…*']

Paul seems to be implying that everything is subject to **Love**.

To the Church in Ephesus

Paul pens a written prayer to this congregation he loves and oversees, and what it is that he is desires for them: [21]

Firstly, to be rooted and grounded in Love.

Secondly, to grasp the vastness of Christ's Love which surpasses knowledge.

---

[20] Colossians 3:14

[21] Read Ephesians 3:14-19 – a stunning prayer.

Thirdly, to actually have a personal knowledge of this Love by being filled with the fullness of God.

Out of everything he could have prayed for them, it's Love!
It seems that every church he's involved with, Love is all around!

Finally, Back to Corinth
After the great Love chapter in the middle of the first letter to the Corinthians, Paul returns once again right at the end with a huge, sweeping, concluding statement:

*'Let **all** that you do be done in Love.'*
NKJV [22]

Hang on - 'all' we do?

That's everything, isn't it?

This is really getting serious!!

---
[22] 1 Corinthians 16:14

THE SECOND MOVEMENT

So you beat the child. Sent him away. Beauty defiled
I love you anyway
You tricked the King. Cut him where he lay. Unthinkable thing
I love you anyway
You held the jewel and you let it fall. Prince of a fool!
I love you most of all

'Love Anyway' by Mike Scott

10. I WANT TO KNOW WHAT LOVE IS 1984

So, if Love is the foundation stone; if it really all comes down to Love and if by Loving God and Loving others we fulfil everything necessary, and if Love needs to be the basis of **all** we do, the big question has to be:

What is Love?

I mean what is it really?
What does it look like?
What does it mean for you and I in the 21st century?
How do I know if I Love, am Loved or am in Love?

Let us begin our journey to try and comprehend this thing called Love.

HAVE A GO

If I were to ask you what, in your opinion, are the three most important words, what would you say?

Before I reveal mine, I actually did an internet search on "the three most important words".

There were, as expected, a wide range of opinions.

Here are just a few:

'I Was Wrong'
'Yes I Can'
'Love, Knowledge, Wisdom'
'I Really Appreciate'
'Be, Do, Have'
'I Love You'
'Attitude, Attitude, Attitude'
'Forgive, Forget, Smile'
'Faith, Hope, Love'

Some thought-provoking responses here. Maybe your choice tallied with one of the above or perhaps yours was totally different.

For me however, the most important three words were written by John the Apostle. John was one of Jesus' original 12 disciples, another significant contributor to the Bible book collection. He wrote 4 New Testament books: 1 gospel and 3 letters.
The latter are called (wait for it…) 1 John, 2 John and (…. yes, you've got it) …3 John.

In the fourth chapter of 1 John, we find this simple, three word phrase: 'GOD IS LOVE'.

He then repeats the phrase again in the same chapter.

Let's just stop and let this sink in (or have what the Bible sometimes calls a *'selah'* moment [23]).

<u>GOD</u>   <u>IS</u>   <u>LOVE</u>

What does that mean?

Well maybe we could put it like this...

God is a Faithful God, but John didn't say God is Faithfulness! God is a God of Hope, but John didn't say God is Hope itself. God is a Merciful God but John didn't say God is Mercy...

but John wrote God **IS** LOVE.

That is who He is.

That is His being, His nature, His make-up. That is His DNA.

---

[23] Selah is a Hebrew word found frequently in the Old Testament book of Psalms. It is thought to mean 'Stop and Listen', or 'Pause and Meditate on'. As many Psalms were put to music it may also be a musical term signifying a break, pause or rest in the song.

So, *whatever this thing called love is - God is it.*

It's a bit early to put a spanner in the works but somehow, whilst that fact may give a reason for the importance placed on Love in the New Testament, it hardly makes the quest of understanding Love any easier. If anything, it adds a dimension that may leave us more confused than ever about what Love is!

11. WHAT IS LOVE? 1984

I want to make two statements around the 'God is Love' phrase, and then follow on by introducing two important words.

Firstly, the two statements.
I'm going to throw out these statements as questions for you to 'selah' (check out that last footnote). Then we'll leave them and move on, and revisit later. Cruel I know, but here we go anyway.

Question Number 1
The New Testament states Jesus is the exact representation of the Father.[24] So if God is Love and Jesus is the exact representation of His being then can we conclude that Jesus is Love, and can we say that if we want to know what Love is, we can look at Jesus?

Question number 2
The Bible also states that we as humans are made in the image and likeness of God. [25] So, If God is Love and we are made in the image of God then can we conclude that we are Love, and can we

---

[24] Hebrews 1:3 – we'll look at this verse later on.
[25] Genesis 1:26

say that if we want to know what Love is, we can look in the mirror?

Let's quickly move on before our heads explode. We will return to these two questions in due course.

Now onto these two important words that will help us in determining what Love is.

12. WORDS OF LOVE 1957

By the way, did I mention the two words were in an old form of Greek no longer in use?

Whilst I can fully understand that this can seem a little off-putting, don't let it be a dampener - there is a reason.

The New Testament was written originally in an ancient form of Common Greek sometimes known as Hellenistic Greek (referring to the historic period between Alexander the Great's death and the birth of the Roman Empire)[26].

It was a rich language and has many words which are difficult to pinpoint as an English equivalent. The two words we are investigating are however, both fairly simple and straight forward because they are both commonly translated into English from the Greek as 'Love'.

The first is the word **EROS**.

The second is the word **AGAPE**.

---

[26] Whilst termed a 'dead' language (as in no longer officially in use), modern day Greek does have many similarities. See Appendix B for more on the Biblical language and history.

Now please don't get the idea that by rabbiting on about Greek, that you are reading the literary work of a great language scholar.[27]

Far from it. [28]

I can however, use a computer mouse and with a couple of clicks in the right direction, I have found it is not that hard to discover the English meaning of words from the original languages that the Bible was written in (namely Hebrew in the Old Testament and Greek in the New Testament).

There are a number of excellent free online Bible programs that can easily be accessed. [29]

---

[27] The only language I took at school was French. I got a U in my GCSE (then called O levels). Under this grading system, A, B & C were passes, D & E were fails and U stood for unclassified - a polite way of saying, there's no point in marking the paper!

[28] A lovely lady in the London Church I pastored, whose late husband was a Greek Professor, lecturer, scholar and author, offered me lessons to learn the language to help my understanding. She had no doubt cringed at my occasional sad attempts to pronounce a Greek word in my sermons, and so I agreed with the proviso that if it got too much, I could withdraw. Much to her disappointment, I lasted 5 weeks!

[29] For example, check out the Blue Letter Bible (www.blueletterbible.org), Biblehub (biblehub.com) or Bible Gateway (www.biblegateway.com).

So, let's read on and delve in turn into these two Greek words of Love.

13. LOVESEXY 1988

The first of the two words is **'Eros'**.

If you've been to Piccadilly Circus, you will know that right in the centre of the circus is a statue, almost an angel like figure with wings aloft, elegantly standing on one leg with a bow in hand. This is none other than the Greek God of love: 'Eros'.

In mythology, Eros was the son of Aphrodite, a goddess associated with sexual love. In early Greek poetry and art, Eros also was depicted as a handsome male embodying love, athleticism, and sexual power. It was believed he had the ability to shoot his magical bow and arrow and make people fall in love with each other.[30]

Bible scholars have debated for centuries a notable fact. Namely why the word 'Eros', being the most common word for 'Love' in the Greek language, is not found **at all** in the New Testament.

The status of Eros as a leading Greek Deity is one possible explanation. Another is of course, that

---

[30] An article from 2017 on Greek Gods & Goddesses is an eye opener. You can find it here - http://greekgodsandgoddesses.net

Eros is traditionally associated with sexuality – it's where the word 'erotic' comes from.

However, whilst it's true that sexuality fits well into 'Eros', the word in itself is not primarily sexual. Eros is probably best described as a love that is immersed in 'self' – a self-focused, self-desire or self-centred love that seeks self-satisfaction.

14. YOU GIVE LOVE A BAD NAME 1986

Now, whilst Eros is not named in the New Testament as a word, the pages are full of Eros as an outworked nature.

In fact, some well-known passages deal with Eros and it is interesting to see the different words that the various English versions use in translating the manifestation of Eros.

Here are a few of the words and phrases from various translations, which show how Eros love has been 'named' in Bible texts:

'Desires of the Flesh' [31]
'Corrupt' [32]
'Selfish Ambition' [33]
'Carnal Mind' [34]
'Earthly Nature' [35]
'Old Way of Life...rotten through and through' [36]

---

[31] Galatians 5:16 NIV
[32] 1 Timothy 6:5 NLT
[33] Philippians 2:3 NIV
[34] Romans 8:7 NKJV
[35] Colossians 3:5 NIV
[36] Ephesians 4:22 TM

For some of you more familiar with the Bible, some of these phrases may be recognisable. You may even know the passages where they can be found. Yet to associate them with a word meaning 'Love' seems the least likely concept ever!

However, I invite you to allow this association as we investigate further

15. SCARY LOVE 2018

There's no doubt about it, when Eros manifests it can be rather scary, but here's something even more frightening.

The way we use the word 'love' in our everyday English language is very much akin to Eros. Think about it - we bandy the word 'love' around in a wide-ranging form. I may say to my wife or my child 'I love you' but I also say I love my cat, I love my new car, I love chocolate ice cream and I love Chelsea Football club. [37]

So, when we say 'I love', what we really mean is 'I strongly like'.

So, in using the word love, I am likely to mean one or more of the statements below:
- I feel warm emotions or positive feelings towards the person or object I 'love.'
- I am attracted towards the person or object I 'love' - they are/ it is pleasing to the eye.
- There is value in the person or object I 'love'. They are/it is useful to me or they/it registers on my value system gauge.

---

[37] One of these is clearly not right...yes you know don't you – I mean we all know strawberry ice cream is better than chocolate!!

- My needs are met (physically or emotionally or spiritually) in the person or object I love.

Can you see that in the way we use love, there is always a return for me? I will not 'love' if I don't like or if there is no benefit to me. It's a self-centred love by nature!

16. YOU'VE LOST THAT LOVIN' FEELING 1964

Have you ever known a couple who met, fell instantly 'in love', became besotted with one another, spent every second of each day possible with each other and announced a quick short engagement?
Suddenly, in no time they are married.

However, a few years later (or shorter) down the track, you find out they have split up, which bodes the question:

How did a couple who were so head over heels in love, so absorbed with each other and with so much passion and energy in their relationship, arrive at separation?

And then you find out the reason...you hear it from a mutual friend or maybe you bump into one of the couple and hear these words directly:
'...we just didn't love each other anymore...'

"Didn't love each other anymore?"

What do they mean?
Probably one or more of the following things:

- The warm fuzzy feelings that once ran riot no longer exist.
- The attraction that once magnetically drew one to the other, now no longer does.
- Personality traits that were different which were attractive at the outset, became over time annoying incompatibilities.
- 'Needs' aren't being met anymore in the same way they once seemed to be, so a dissatisfaction is growing.

And there it is: 'Eros' in full attire!

'I love'...sure I do - but ultimately, it's about what I get out of it.

That 'love' is based on self-fulfillment and self-satisfaction.
Eros is ego-centric. Man centered.

It's what we can call 'human love' because that is at root level how 'love' generally works in day-to-day life. It is how society ticks.

Now let me just point out that this is a human condition. It is human nature. We are all tarred with the same brush. None of us are exempt.

Although many would not acknowledge that or even be aware of it, the truth is (as uncomfortable as it may make us) in our natural human state, self is the object to be satisfied.

We are Eros through and through.

17. TAINTED LOVE 1981

Now let's balance things before we unbalance things.

Eros is not bad or evil in itself.

As human beings we were created with needs. It's natural to desire food when you're hungry; sexual appetites are normal; it's good to attribute value and worth to different things.

But the reality is that Eros is a very powerful force. That means it can so easily become tainted.

Unless it's governed, it will spiral out of control. If there are no restraints, restrictions and boundaries applied to life, Eros will act like a spreading weed in a garden, and will start to run wild.

More and more, the Eros desires will seek to be satisfied as appetites and yearnings grow. More is now needed to quench the expanding hunger, and desires become all consuming.

Suddenly we can find ourselves not only out of control but controlled! At which point Eros is not only self-centered but it becomes self-consuming;

a love that's only purpose is to meet its own needs and desires.

We see examples of this in areas such as power and wealth and status and fame. People will do almost anything to attain their goals.

In addition, once we understand the nature of Eros, we see how the original association of sexuality fits in so aptly with the word. As we've already noted, the English word that has its origin in Eros is of course 'erotic' - it turns me on - it's attractive to look at - it arouses me and I must be satisfied.

Addiction within society today is becoming more widespread, it seems: alcohol, cocaine, gambling, gaming, sugar, shopping, working - the list goes on - but as widespread as these are, I truly believe that the Number 1 addiction today is pornography and related sexual issues.

This has always been an issue but the scale has exploded, thanks to the internet which has generously provided an open doorway and invitation to every home.

The homes I suspect where the door has remained unopened, are well in the minority!

How appropriate one of the Greek words in the New Testament for 'evil' is `porneia` which of course is the source of the word for pornography.

18. HIGHER LOVE 1986

On that cheery note, lets pause and move on to the second Greek word for Love that we want to investigate: **Agape**.

Agape [38] is a word that did not appear in the ancient Greek language until the Gospels and its use initially, was extremely limited outside of scripture.

Yet it is the most common word for Love in the New Testament.

The number of times Love is used, varies from translation to translation but on average, of all the times the word Love is used, around 85% of the time it is the word Agape; in other words, the high majority.

Two of these occasions are the repeated phrase we talked about earlier in John's first letter… 'God is AGAPE'.

So immediately we see this word takes on huge importance.

---

[38] The word is a noun. Obviously, the verb, adverb, tenses etc, have variations on this word, but for simplicity's sake, I'm sticking to 'Agape' for the lot!

This is a higher Love, a Love that is sourced from and through the God of the universe. It has divine origin.

Now straight away, we see an immediate contrast to Eros.

Eros remember is man-centred whereas Agape, we now see is God-centred (or 'theo-centric' if you want the formal lingo).

But that understanding immediately reminds us of a potentially huge challenge that we touched on before:

To what extent can we realistically expect to understand Agape, bearing in mind we are trying to define a word that is the very DNA of God?

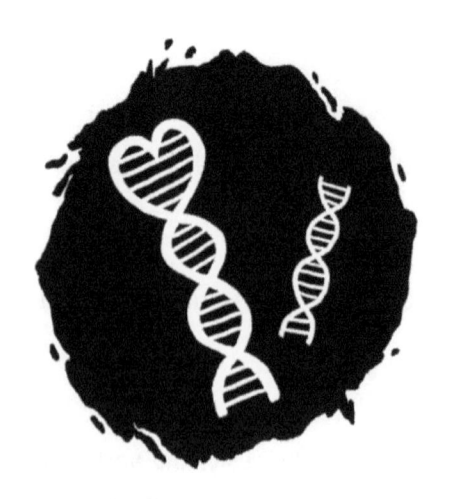

Well, I'm not sure about an adequate definition, but we can certainly know Agape and this is thanks to John and his first letter again.

Let's follow where he takes us.

19. THE LOOK OF LOVE 1982

Let me first tell you a brief story and in doing so 'paint a picture…'

Imagine you get invited to a special event at an Art Gallery where a famous artist is unveiling a new painting:
It is called 'Love'.
There is enormous hype and excitement over this latest work. Yet all the talking over what it may be or look like is really irrelevant. It is not until the grand opening when the artist pulls the cord and the curtains open to reveal the painting, that the true magnificence of the artwork can be understood. Only then can 'Love' really be seen in all its glory.
As you look and contemplate the depths of the painting, you start to become aware of the structure of the composition, the beauty of the image, the harmony of the colours, the intricacy of the design, the fineness of the brushstrokes, all working together to convey the simple powerful message of what this picture called 'Love' is about.

As you gaze in wonder, you begin to understand that this work has truly come from within the depths of the artist himself and you get a glimpse of the cost and investment it must have taken to produce.

It dawns on you the longer you immerse yourself in the picture that you are in the presence of a true masterpiece!

So, after this supreme declaration in 1 John 4 verse 8 that 'God is Agape', it's like in the very next verse he pulls the cord to reveal the picture. We read in the next two verses, 9 and 10;

'God showed his love for us when he sent his only Son into the world to give us life. Real Love isn't our Love for God, but His Love for us. God sent his Son to be the sacrifice by which our sins are forgiven.' CEV

If you look closely at these two verses, you will notice a three-fold demonstration here:

First, we can see an **Act** of Love: God showed Agape by the act of sending His Son for our sin...there's a well-known song sung in churches which has a bridge which goes *'I'll never know how much it costs, to see my sin upon the cross.'* [39]

Second, there's an **Appearance** of Love: God showed Agape in the person of Jesus.

Third, notice a **Comparison** of Love: God showed that Agape Love is very different from what man thinks of as love. It suggests that real Love isn't our love but His Love.

---

[39] 'Light of the World' written by Tim Hughes © Copyright 2001 Thankyou Music

In other words, in the context of what we've been looking at, we could say that real Love is not derived from man (Eros) but real Love is sourced from God (Agape).

So, we can start to see that God's plan to make Agape known is centred around the person of Jesus.

This is all well and good but how does this help us in identifying Agape in day-to-day life?

I mean Jesus doesn't walk the earth today so it's not like we can go and see him or ask him, is it?

So how do I recognise it practically?

Let's begin with the basics.

If you have ever heard a sermon in church on Love where the word 'Agape' has been identified by the speaker, the chances are it would be defined as 'Unconditional Love'.

In other words, if I love (Agape), I do so without any conditions attached.

This is a 'Love 101' definition of Agape.

Let's now try and deepen our understanding by building on this definition; we can do this by introducing another picture illustration, which will help us in our comprehension of both types of Love:

Agape and Eros.[40]

---

[40] Without wanting to complicate matters, it's worth noting at this point there are other Greek words translated as 'Love' in the New Testament. One is the word 'Phileo' which indicates a deep friendship, affection or often referred to as brotherly love (hence 'Philadelphia', the city of brotherly love). Another is the word 'Storge' which indicates the love of a family or the instinctive love a parent has for a child. We will not be dealing with these any further in this book.

20. LOVE IS AN ARROW 2005

This illustration was used by Bob Mumford in our 'conference' tape series 'Unshared Love'. [41] It helped both Kirsten and I to grasp the essence of both Agape and Eros, and I hope it will for you.

I remember when Bob first introduced this idea in the tape set, he made this rather bold statement:

'All of life reduces to 2 arrows'.

I remember thinking at the time, 'Now, this *will* be interesting,' as a degree of doubt and scepticism crept into my mind.

But you know what? Having lived with this now for many years and observed life …oh my goodness, he's right!

These 2 arrows represent the 2 types of love we've looked at:

---

[41] Also covered in Bob's books 'The Agape Road - Journey to Intimacy with the Father' and 'Mysterious Seed' (Destiny Image 2006 & 2011 respectively).

Agape: Divine Love - represented by a straight arrow

Eros: Human Love - represented by a bent or hooked arrow

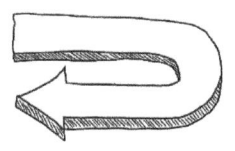

Let's look at each in turn:

21. (THIS ONE GOES OUT TO) THE ONE I LOVE 1987

Let's first look at Agape using the illustration of the first arrow.

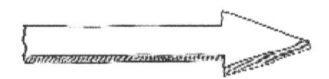

Imagine you visit an archery range. You hire a bow and some arrows and step up to the shooting line. You see the target in the distance and you know your goal is the bullseye, the inner most circle of the target (although if it were me, any part of the target I hit would be a victory!).

You take aim,

slowly pull back the string,

and then you fire the arrow.

Agape is just like that arrow. It is launched by the one who Loves and goes out to the one who is Loved, in a perfect, undeviating straight line. It has no expectations of the target. It simply seeks to be received into the heart of the target.

The condition of the target is irrelevant – it is not based on how it looks, its value, its quality, or its history, nor does the one Loving expect anything in return from the one Loved. There are no conditions, demands or expectations of getting anything back (hence unconditional Love).

Its goal is just to reach and embed in the target.

Paul, in his letter to the Romans, gives a perfect example:

'God demonstrated his own Love (Agape) for us in this: while we were sinners Christ died for us.' NIV [42]

This verse provides an actual demonstration of Agape. God fired the arrow. His target was every individual that has been uniquely created (including you).

---

[42] Romans 5:8

Take note that when He fired that Agape arrow, He didn't wait until we were nice, or had prayed, or had our act cleaned up, or were a regular church attender. It was at a time when we had turned our backs on God, through ignorance, unbelief or rebellion. It was at a time when our hearts and minds were totally absorbed in pursuing self-gain. It was at this time He sent His Son to die for us!

No hidden agendas!

No conditions!

No expectations!

What a wonderful demonstration of Agape

...and that is **exactly** how God loves you!

22. I WILL DO ANYTHING FOR LOVE BUT I WON'T DO THAT 1993

Now let's look at the second arrow in comparison. The hooked arrow of Eros.

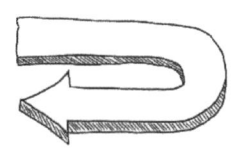

Remember the nature of Eros under the 'Lovesexy' Song Chapter 13? Love is totally conditional - it is based on whether something is pleasing or attractive or valuable or useful or satisfying.

Remember, I only love what I strongly like.

Yes, I'll love you as long as…but if I don't like it or it doesn't do it for me, I can't/won't love.

So, Eros is like a boomerang arrow - it has return in it! In other words, when I love Eros, I fire it towards the person or object I love but its final goal (whether I'm aware of it or not) is actually back at me.

This is love with a hook!

So, there are our 2 arrows!

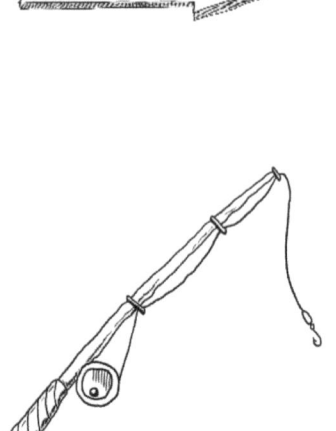

AND

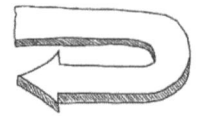

It's a bit like visiting a pond with fish in it. I can take some bread to give to the fish. I may stand on the edge and simply throw the pieces of bread in. My goal is nothing other than to feed the fish.

But I could put that bread on a hook. I'm still feeding the fish but now I'm after something. The fish are not aware of any difference initially... until they take the bread.

You get the idea.

But what about the claim that all of life comes down to these arrows? Well, the application of these arrows to everyday life is widespread. I want to show you several areas of application but firstly think about this:

In our day-to-day lives, we perform lots of actions and activities, many of which involve other people. Some we know well and are in close relationship with (family/ friends/ work colleagues) and others we may not know well at all or even could be meeting for the first time (business client, new neighbour, first date).

With every interaction there is give and take. In other words, sometimes we undertake actions that result in us giving to others, and sometimes we do things that end up with us taking or receiving.

Think for a moment of giving being the straight arrow, and receiving being the hooked arrow. Now think of two levels or dimensions, an outer, physical, external seen part and an inner spiritual, internal, unseen part.

Now it is perfectly natural and normal for everyday life to be a mixture of giving and taking physically. For example, I may hire a contractor to do a repair on my house and I pay him. For me, I receive his skill and knowledge, and I give him money. For him he gets paid but he has given me of his time and abilities. This is one simple example of many day-to-day interactions to which the 2 arrows can be applied.

But the real power of the arrows takes place at the inner unseen level – in a person's heart and mind, sometimes referred to as the soul or spirit. This involves the attitudes and intentions of the real 'you'.

For example, Paul teaches this in his letter to the Philippians encouraging them to be *'not looking to your own interests but each of you to the interests of the others'* NIV.[43]

Paul is not talking of external interactions here but the heart motivation of what is really going on. He is encouraging an Agape way of life in our relationships with others…to always look to be a giver and not just a taker.

Read the Philippians verse one more time. Can you see the two arrows here together in this one verse? In 'arrow language' Paul is saying when you are dealing with others, have a straight arrow and not a hooked one!

---

[43] Philippians 2:4. He then goes on to show Jesus as the ultimate example of one who was a giver, and challenges the readers of the letter to be the same.

23. I SEE LOVE EVERYWHERE I LOOK 2016

Since becoming aware of the 2 arrows, I have developed a hobby. I like to call it '*The Fine Art Of Arrow Spotting*'. It is a bit like train spotting but arguably not so geeky!

I would point out it is extremely compelling because if you look with intention, you won't need to go very far to spot the arrows. In fact, you'll start to see them all over the place, especially the hooked ones, and you'll start [like me] to begin to believe Bob Mumford's claim!

To get you going, here are 5 potential guideline areas to develop and hone your ability to 'arrow spot'.

▱▱▱▷ **Firstly,** you will spot them **in the Bible.**

You are already underway with this one. I've given you a kick start with the Philippians verse above. The Bible really is a fascinating arena for arrow spotting especially as, if you remember, the word 'Eros' isn't found as an actual pure word. Yet as we've already stated, the principle of Eros is everywhere through its pages.[44]

I have a Bible where several years ago, I began to mark in the margin, either a straight or hooked arrow against a verse where I spotted Agape or Eros at work. Flicking through the pages now, I am amazed at the extent of my 'artwork'. There are arrows everywhere.

But I shouldn't be surprised. In many ways, the Bible in its rawness, is an account of God right throughout history, seeking to meet Eros infected man, in the midst of his ever-changing culture and times, through an outpouring of Agape. In other words, it is the story of 2 arrows.

HAVE A GO

Let's do a bit of arrow-spotting together by looking at a passage as an example.

---

[44] I am aware that not all readers of this book will be readers of the Bible and if not, don't worry, there'll be plenty of opportunity elsewhere. But to get the idea, you may want to try the 'Have a Go' above.

Find a Bible, either a hard copy or an online version and find Luke Chapter 6. Then scroll down to verse 27.

Jesus is teaching on Love and starts off 'Love (Agape) your enemies (there's a straight arrow) and do good to those who hate you (straight arrow again).' [45]

Immediately we see 2 arrows in one verse.

Now read for yourself, verse 28 through to verse 36 and see how many other straight or hooked arrows you can spot.

Of course, the Bible is not the only source of arrow-spotting.

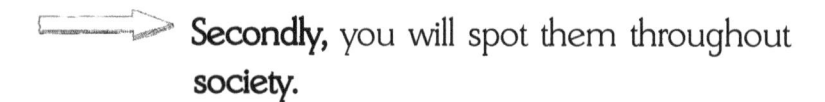

➡ **Secondly,** you will spot them throughout **society.**

Switch on the news or pick up the daily papers and read a few articles; chances are it won't be long before you spot a few arrows.

---

[45] By the way, I always struggled with these verses. How can you possibly love your enemies and do good to those who hurt you? It only became clear to me when I realised the word for 'Love' is Agape and I understood the straight arrow!

You'll notice that they appear through all areas of society – politics, business, education, entertainment, sports, etc.

Jesus said in Matthew 24:12 – *'Sin will be rampant everywhere, and the Love (Agape) of many will grow cold.'* NLT

'Sin' is a word that is not popular today, but for me it's a great word because at the centre of the word is the letter 'I' which is the very root of the sin disease.

Think of all the crimes and wrongdoings that exist – stealing, lying, cheating, etc. Whatever it is, you can always trace it back to self and a hooked arrow: self-gratification, self-preservation, self-promotion, self-advancement…etc. So, the Bible verse above works brilliantly because it could be paraphrased:

'As the 'I' disease" of Eros increases, Agape is quenched.'

24. THIS AIN'T A LOVE SONG (THIS IS GOODBYE) 2010

If you want proof of an Eros rise and Agape decline, simply look at how the basic foundation of society has changed over the last 150 years or so.

150 years ago in Western Society, there was predominantly a 'Christian' culture and influence. Most people went to church, and had basic Bible knowledge. People had good manners and children learnt to respect their elders.

But gradually and very subtly, there crept in a series of influential philosophies and new ideas that gradually took root. With ideologies from individuals such as Karl Marx, Charles Darwin and Sigmund Freud in the 19th century, an alternative focus came into people's awareness, concentrating on the material world, suggesting our universe could exist without God. The Secular Humanism movement followed in the first half of the 20th century promoting human reason, natural laws and secular ethics as the basis of morality, replacing any religious dogma, supernaturalism or spirituality.

As we've seen, when God is pushed out, Agape will grow cold and Eros, the self-centred culture, evolves.

That was exactly what happened with the emergence of the 'entitlement movement' from the 1960s onwards - everyone demanding what they want and what they felt entitled to - right now! This has spiralled out of control as the kingdom of Eros has thrived, and the damage has become widespread, reaching global epidemic proportions.

Thankfully, in the early part of the 21st century, society, it seems, has gradually woken up to the very real threat to our planet; there has been a dawning awareness of the need to change. There has also been a realisation that the start of the solution lies with the necessity of man to look outside himself.

This is proof indeed that an Eros lifestyle, if left unchallenged, takes us down the pathway that is the real highway to hell. If allowed to mature, this 'self' disease will eventually arrive at its inevitable destination:

Self-Destruction:

Personally.
Nationally.
Globally.

This ain't no love song!

⟹ **Thirdly** you'll spot them in day-to-day **relationships.**

Take any relationship where there is a closeness:

Husband / Wife
Child /Parent
Boyfriend / Girlfriend
Employer/ Employee
Congregation/ Pastor

Now let's apply the arrows relationally using the list above, in a couple of scenarios:

A ⟸ ⟵   B ⟸ ⟹

Let's say in both scenarios, the first arrow is the first mentioned of the pair (i.e. the husband, the child, etc) and the second arrow is the second mentioned of the pair (i.e. the wife, the parent, etc).

In scenario A, the first of the pair is the recipient of Agape - they are being loved simply because they are who they are. But they have an agenda. They are after something at this point in the relationship and there is a hidden agenda that seeks a personal desire or goal. Take a boyfriend / girlfriend relationship. He says 'I love you'. She responds 'I love you'. But he is after something. Any guesses what that may be?

Of course, it can be the other way round too.

In scenario B, Eros meets Eros. In other words, each party has a motive that is hidden. A pastor arranges a visit to a member of the congregation. *'I just wanted to see how you're settling into the church'* says the pastor, wondering when will the right time be to drop into the conversation that the church cleaning roster has some gaps. *'I like it much better than my last church because of the way you use different people in the Sunday services'* comes the reply, with a plan to use this opportunity to suggest that they have a preaching gift and would be willing to 'help out anytime'.

From time to time, you may spot arrows whilst observing a relational interaction. This is very obvious in fictional relationships portrayed on the TV, especially the soaps. It's quite fun to watch one episode and see how many arrows you spot, especially the hooked ones.

But there will be times in real life situations when you discern relational arrows in use. It's not that you want to. You just do. In these scenarios it's important not to judge.

⟹ **Fourthly** you'll spot them in **church.**

It would be nice to think the church was immune, but oh my goodness, it seems at times, the church leads the Eros charge!

Whether it's people leaving churches because they don't like the worship leader's style
or
new Christians moving away from the faith because God hasn't answered their prayers in the way they want
or
scriptures being twisted and used Eros style to achieve an outcome
or
church splits due to doctrinal disagreements with each side believing they're right [46]
or
pastoral visits with ulterior motives as in the example above.

Sadly, the hooks are everywhere. I'm not being cynical here, just real, knowing that none of us are immune.

And really nothing's changed. Going back to the first church, Paul's 'Eros encounters' are well

---

[46] All churches have annual general meetings, some have annual general splits!

documented; for example, taking advantage of weaker people,[47] looking for personal advantage,[48] or highlighting ingrained Eros behaviour to the Ephesian Church [49] or even preaching Christ out of selfish ambition. [50]

Oh, and one more area where you'll encounter some arrows…

⟶ **Fifthly** you'll spot them **in you.**

I'm afraid you will never achieve a distinction in the hobby of arrow spotting unless you turn the spotlight on your own ways, interactions and reactions. It's one thing to spot arrows from other people and situations, it's another when you spot them coming from you, especially if they have a hook in them.

I have been shocked at how many hooked arrows I fire without even realising it's happening. It sometimes seems like it is my default mode! An

---

[47] Romans 16:17,18

[48] 1 Corinthians 10:33

[49] Ephesians 4:17-32

[50] Philippians 1:15-16 – If you're a preacher, you know you can 'phrase things' to make yourself look good before others, or even preach to make yourself feel good. Lots of potential nasties tied in with this.

Agape understanding has revealed that so much of my 'loving' is not Agape.

Maybe that is the whole point.

It means of course, that I have had to face the conclusion, uncomfortable as it is, that I am part of the problem.

If you are honest, so are you!

As disturbing as that is, hold onto your hats because what's coming next could make you even more uncomfortable.

25. LOVE IS A BATTLEFIELD 1983

There's a war going on. We all know it. It has existed since the dawn of time. It's most commonly called the battle of good and evil... and it exists primarily on two levels.

The first is the cosmic battle – we could view it as God vs Satan or Angels vs Demons or Love vs Hate.

The second is personal. We know that this very battle goes on to some degree within each of us.

As human beings we tend to be very black and white in our thinking. It's either this...or it's that. The term for this is dualistic thinking, and it can be dangerous, because we can judge people and situations, according to our 'Eros' nature. For example, if someone has an alternative viewpoint, we may think we are right and they are wrong.

Dualistic thinking can occur in the battle of good and evil. Movies do a great job in formulating clearly defined 'goodies' and 'baddies'.

But real life isn't really like that, is it?

You see there really aren't good people and bad people. We're all a mixture.

One of my wife's favourite quotes is from **Solzhenitsyn,** who whilst in a prison camp wrote:

"Gradually it was disclosed to me that the line separating good and evil passes not through states, nor between classes, nor between political parties either – but right through every human heart – and through all human hearts. This line shifts. Inside us, it oscillates with the years. And even within hearts overwhelmed by evil, one small bridgehead of good is retained. And even in the best of all hearts, there remains... an un-uprooted small corner of evil." [51]

---

[51] Aleksandr Solzhenitsyn: The Gulag Archipelago, Part 4, Chapter 1, "The Ascent" (1973 Editions du seuil).

So exists the battle for the human heart within each one of us. We could view it as Good vs Evil, Spiritual vs Carnal, or Heavenly vs Earthly, but as we are start to get a grasp on the nature of these two ancient Greek words, perhaps Agape vs Eros is another helpful way to view and understand this internal conflict.

So, with a battle mode mentality, let's do an Agape vs Eros summary on what we've discovered so far, by comparing the two types of love and how each of the two line up.

EROS SUMMARY	AGAPE SUMMARY
HUMAN Origin	DIVINE Origin
MAN Centred	GOD Centred
SELF Focused	OTHERS Focused
CONDITIONAL: Based on attractiveness, arousal, value, status, reputation, positive feeling, warm emotions, needs met, desires satisfied, gain/ return for me	UNCONDITIONAL: Not based on attractiveness, arousal, value, status, reputation, positive feeling, warm emotions, needs met, desires satisfied, gain/ return for me

When you see simplified summaries of each standing side by side, we can see something obvious. We see that not only are the two types of love different from each other but *actually virtually opposite in their nature and outworking.*

The nature of each is in direct conflict with the other. It is like the battle-lines are drawn.

Now I promised to make you uncomfortable, and so here goes.

Remember way back in Song Chapter 7 where we started looking at Love when Jesus summarised the whole Old Testament stating, 'All you Need is Love'? In other words, Jesus was saying, `If you Love God and Love others, you've cracked the whole deal!`.

We can now get an insight as to what Jesus is actually doing here. He is introducing a new way of loving and living, which is Agape. We can also see by referring to the summary chart on the last page, that if we decide to live in this new way, it is the opposite way of living to what we are naturally used to.

Now think about this. Without an Agape understanding (which most people, including Christians don't have), can you see how easy it is to read Jesus' words and just default into the love we know, which is Eros based?

This effectively means we can end up responding to Jesus's teaching by immediately setting off down the wrong path, and begin to live the opposite of how he is encouraging us to live!

I don't know how you react to that, but to me it is a frightening thought.

So, let's not dwell on it - let's be positive and have a go at a personal exercise.

HAVE A GO

Find a quiet place. Be still for a few moments.

Then ask yourself this question: how do I love those around me?

Reflect on the last 24 hours! Think about conversations, interactions and encounters. What were your thoughts, attitudes, motivations behind them? Any hidden agendas? Were you looking for a return? Do you spot any hooks?

In addition, if you're a person of faith...think of your thoughts, contemplations and prayers with the Divine? Does your love for Him fluctuate with how well your life is going? When you talk to Him, do you seek approval or to prove something?

To what capacity can you and do you love God with Eros?

Now as you go into the next 24 hours, try and maintain an awareness - make an effort to observe yourself today.

This may be uncomfortable. In fact, I hope it is, because it's the arrow spotting in your own life and relationships that will be the catalyst to cause you to desire to change.

For me the realisation that I was so far off the mark and that I had more hooks than a professional fisherman, caused me to fall on my knees and admit I was deeply infected by Eros and could not see a way through.

I knew that the answer was not trying harder. Trying to love with Agape out of my own strength and ability was always going to be doomed to failure.

I needed help...and somehow that help needed to come from an outside source!

26. LOVE ME TENDER 1957

God is Agape. Agape is His pure nature. It is His DNA.

Love received from God cannot be anything other than Agape because that is who He is!

I don't know about you but I am so very pleased that God loves me with Agape and not Eros. Otherwise, we would all be in big trouble.

But the question we are dealing with now is what hope is there for me? Is there an outside source of help that can lead me forward in the way of Agape, but not only that, to empower me to live it daily?

Well for me, a glimmer of hope first came through the writings of St Augustine.

Augustine of Hippo was a Catholic bishop and theologian in AD300s - 400s. [I like him because among other things he is the patron saint of brewers! How cool is that?]

The first thing I discovered was that this same issue that we are wrestling with right here and now, was also being wrestled with way back then. [I don't know why I should be surprised. There is nothing new under the sun and so if anything is important today, you can bet it was back then!]

St Augustine in his contemplations over Love [52] came to some interesting conclusions, which I found really helpful.

Firstly, he concluded that the way of all human love, even our love for God is acquisitive. In other words, it seeks to acquire. So, for example, when we come to God, we always want to improve our lives. We want to be happier, live better, or we ask for blessing, seek healing and look to satisfy our own spiritual hunger through prayer.

Secondly; he concluded that this in itself wasn't necessarily wrong, because it is in God's nature and heart to want to bless and heal and satisfy us too. He wants the best for our lives just as we do.

Thirdly; he concluded that the key aspect of the difference between human love (Eros) and Agape is in its purpose or goal. *Agape's goal does not lie in things but in relationship.* So, the goal of God's Love for me is rooted in His desire for intimacy, for

---

[52] St Augustine's Love Sermon -
https://christianhistoryinstitute.org/study/module/augustine

fellowship, for communion. It is a gentle, tender, deep and intensely personal Love.

That was a major revelation for me.

27. THE POWER OF LOVE
1984/1985/ 1985/1994 [4 points]

The lightbulb flickered for a while and then eventually came on.

For the first time I understood what God really wants from me – simply me.

He seeks what He's always sought: union, relationship, intimacy, one-ness - that's the reason we were created in the first place.

That's why He gave His only Son - because the outpouring of Agape to the world was the way to defeat the Eros 'I' disease.

You see once I am truly aware of Agape and become the recipient of its power, Eros is exposed in my life, and my desire can be nothing other than for change - to embark on the Agape Road - to learn to love as I am designed to love.

So back to the arrows.

Remember the two scenarios we looked at in regard to relationships back in Song Chapter 24?

We can apply similar examples in the area of our relationship with God. This time, let's say the first arrow is me (or you) and the second is God.

A ⊃ ⇐   B ⇒ ⇐

In scenario A, God comes at me with a straight arrow of Agape, whilst I am submerged in my Eros lifestyle.

I may be at a stage in my life where I reject, ignore or deny God. Alternatively, I may accept God is real but I am very much self-absorbed with my life and He plays little or no part in it. A third option could be that I have a real relationship with Him, but my prayers and conversations with God are largely focused on asking for things, and self-fulfilment. All of these can be represented by the hooked arrow.

But God doesn't change. His love never changes. Wherever we are at, His arrows of Agape keep coming, seeking the human heart as a target for His Love to be received.

And He will never give up!

You see I believe God's desire for every one of us is to arrive at scenario B.

This is the place where Agape meets Agape; the point where true intimacy and connection occurs. The journey towards achieving this is threefold:

Firstly, we become aware of His Love,

Secondly, we open our hearts to receive His love

Thirdly, we can respond to His love with love

In other words, I can just love God for who He is just as He loves me for who I am.

I find when I contemplate this, I sense something within me rising up, and yearning for the authentic intimacy that is only possible through Agape.

Maybe you do too.

But mingled in with this desire may also be an aspect of doubt. Is it really possible to have an ongoing closeness with the Living God? Can I truly develop a real relationship of openness and transparency with Him?

The answer I believe, is 'Yes – absolutely'.

I believe it is in fact what we were created for.

I believe it's the journey we are all invited on - a journey to a restoration and true union with God where we can begin to enjoy a genuine friendship and intimacy with our Creator and Father.

A journey where we can know the *real* **Power of Love.**

INTERLUDE

28. STOP! IN THE NAME OF LOVE 1965

We are going to look at the journey just described in more detail in the next section. But first, a brief interlude!

Hopefully your understanding of God's love and the nature of Agape is deepening, along with just how central it is to life and faith.

So, let's just pause on our journey just for a few moments and look at a few more verses in scripture which, when read in the light of Agape, take on a new realm of beauty and meaning.

HAVE A GO

All the words for Love in the verses below are 'Agape'.

Read each verse aloud as written, and then read them aloud again, replacing the word Love with 'Agape', pausing and meditating on each one for a short time.

- *1 Corinthians 14:1* 'Follow the way of **Love**' NIV

- *Romans 13: 8-10* 'Owe no one anything except to **love** one another, for he who **loves** another has fulfilled the law. For the commandments, "You shall not commit adultery", "You shall not murder", "You shall not steal", "You shall not bear false witness", "You shall not covet", and if *there is* any other commandment, are *all* summed up in this saying, namely, "You shall **love** your neighbour as yourself." **Love** does no harm to a neighbour; therefore **love** *is* the fulfilment of the law.' NKJV

- *Ephesians 5:1-2* Imitate God, therefore, in everything you do, because you are his dear children. Live a life filled with **love**, following the example of Christ. He **loved** us and offered himself as a sacrifice for us.' NLT

- *Ephesians 5:25* Husbands, **love** your wives, just as Christ **loved** the church and gave himself up for her.' NIV [53]

---

[53] *This scripture alone is enough to revolutionise a marriage with an Agape revelation.*

- *Galatians 5:13* My friends, you were chosen to be free. So don't use your freedom as an excuse to do anything you want. Use it as an opportunity to serve each other with **love**.' CEV

- *1 John 3:1* 'See what great **love** the Father has lavished on us, that we should be called children of God.' NIV

- *1 Corinthians 16:14* Let **all** that you do be done in **love**.' NKJV

I don't know about you, but for me, these verses take on a whole new dimension of power, tenderness, depth and understanding.

It's good to 'selah' for a while.

But now, let's continue on…

THE THIRD MOVEMENT

'When the big me meets the big you

The things we will do.'

'Love Anyway' by Mike Scott

29. LESSONS IN LOVE 1987

When the revelation of Agape starts to dawn, it really is a wonderful and exciting time. But as is so often the case, discovering some answers to something often leads to more questions. Often these questions follow a natural progression that involve moving from the theoretical to the practical. In other words: I now understand it, but how do I start to apply this?

Right now, you may be in the place where you have a grasp on the nature of Agape. You see the importance of it, you know it is right to pursue it. You may be developing a desire to outlive it but at the same time you are very much aware of Eros alive and kicking within. Maybe you recognise some of those hooked arrows ingrained in you and wonder how you can ever become the person that God (and you) want you to become?

So, the questions now starting to take shape within you may be along the lines of *'How do I start to Agape?'* or *'How do I know if or when I am living out 'Agape?'* or 'How *can I consistently live a life of Agape?'*

Well, for the next stage of our journey, we are going to learn two great lessons, which should move us in a direction that will help us in answering these questions.

Both lessons are foundational to Love and Life today.

The **first lesson** teaches us <u>what Agape looks like</u> practically [covered in the remainder of this Song Chapter 29 & 30].

The **second lesson** teaches us <u>how we can live a life</u> of Agape [We will look at this in Song Chapters 31 to 33].

*So **firstly**, how do I recognise Agape Love right here, right now, today? What does it look like?*

As we look through history at different civilisations, cultures and empires, man has sought to discover the divine and in doing so developed beliefs on how that God or gods acted and responded.

The Bible itself is an account of human history, recording man's encounters and interactions through the ages with what is sometimes referred to as 'the one' or the 'only true' God. [54]

Therefore, through its pages, we read about people like Noah, and Abraham, David and Solomon, among

---

[54] For example: John 17:3, 1 Corinthians 8:6, 1 Timothy 2:5 (KJV)

many others, trying to comprehend and get to grips with who this God was.[55]

In fact, the New Testament book of Hebrews starts by referring to these:

'In the past God spoke to our ancestors through the prophets at many times and in various ways.' [56]

The Amplified Bible in translating this verse, opens up the phrase *'In various ways'* by stating:

*'...in many separate revelations, each of which **set forth a portion** of the truth...'*

Another translation - The International Standard Version - puts it like this:

*'God, having spoken in former times in **fragmentary** and varied fashion...'*

Now that's an interesting thought. God revealed things in portions or in fragments. Piecemeal.

---

[55] In the process of discovery, perceptions of what God was like varied. The fact that God is sometimes portrayed in the Old Testament as a violent almost vengeful God at times, is a difficult subject and a stumbling block for many. I recommend a great book on this topic called 'A More Christlike God by Bradley Jersak *(Plain Truth Ministries 2015)*

[56] Hebrews 1:1 NIV

Maybe we could view it a bit like jigsaw pieces with each piece having just a portion of the complete picture. So, it seems that these Old Testament characters experienced God, but only got fragments of the picture of who God was!

There's a great example involving Moses which can be found in the book of Exodus. [57] *Here Moses is at a point in his life where he's desperate to know God more. He's seen God move using powerful and miraculous works, but now he wants to know* **who** *this God is behind these works!*

One day he cries out in prayer 'God show me your glory'.

The Hebrew word for glory is 'Kavod' which means weight/ substance.

Now Moses is in fact not asking God to reveal His divine weight, but rather His 'substance', His make-up, His nature, His DNA.'

The amazing thing is that God agrees. He tells Moses to climb a mountain and hide in a cleft in the rock while His glory (Kavod) passes by...but God tells him you can't see my face, you'll only see my back.

---

[57] You'll find this account reading from Exodus Chapter 33 v17 through to Chapter 34 v8

How intriguing… so what happens?

Moses does as he's told and God passes by and proclaims:

'I am the Lord, the God of mercy, grace, patience, goodness, forgiveness, truth, justice and Love'.

In other words, God reveals His glory; His nature, His DNA, who he really is, His 'Kavod'. But not all of it- just part of it – just a fragment, a portion - in fact His backside.

Still, not bad for a rear view, don't you think?

Now, if we go back to the start of Hebrews and read the next couple of verses, you will see something of vital importance.

Following verse 1 which tells us that God spoke in the past to our ancestors in various ways (portions/ fragments), we now read:

'but in these last days he has spoken to us by his Son, whom he appointed heir of all things, and through whom also he made the universe. The Son is the

radiance of God's glory and the exact representation of his being. '[58]

Do you remember earlier in the book (Song Chapter 11), I posed two questions and kind of left you pondering, saying I would return to them in due time? Well, it is time to return to the first of the two questions, which was:

If God is love (Agape) and Jesus is the exact representation of His being (as the verse above states) then can we conclude that Jesus is Love (Agape)?

I believe the answer to this is a resounding *'YES.'*

Note Hebrews 1:3 says two things:

First that Jesus is the **radiance of God's glory.** The Greek word 'radiance' indicates an almost pulsating source of energy or light. Some versions translate the word 'brightness'.

The picture is that Jesus radiated / pulsated with intensity, the substance, the nature, the DNA of His Father.

---

[58] Hebrews 1:2-3 NIV

Second, that He is the **exact representation** of His being. The Greek wording here implies a photographic image, just like say a passport photo would exactly represent you and suffice for ID.

There's an incident recorded in John's gospel where Phillip, one of the twelve disciples, comes to Jesus and asks Jesus to show them the Father.[59]

I can imagine Jesus, kind of lovingly shaking his head, as He delivers His response (paraphrased): *'Phillip don't you get it…you've been with me the whole time and you're still missing it …if you're looking at me or listening to me, then you are witnessing the Father.'*

Of course, this was a key reason that Jesus, the Son came to earth and took on human form. He came to show us the Father, to reveal the true nature of God. He came to put an end to the opinions and confusion over the centuries, as to what God was like and how He operated.

---

[59] You'll find this in John 14

In Jesus, the fragments have all come together and at last we have a true picture of the Divine. An 'exact likeness' of God.

'Anyone who has seen me' said Jesus *'has seen the Father.'* [60]

---

[60] John 14:9 NIV

30. TRUE LOVE 2013

We are starting to learn our first lesson in Love. We are able to identify Agape at work in a human body in the person of Jesus and see it being outworked in flesh and blood. Jesus is the exact representation of God's nature, the same DNA and therefore a true representation of Love. Jesus is Agape personified.

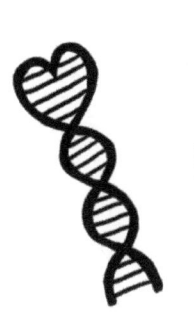

We could say He was the first person in human flesh to show us what it means to live and love with a straight arrow.

Now to really understand this, let's hold up what we've learnt so far in the light of the great 'Love Chapter' of 1 Corinthians 13.

You may recall back in Song Chapter 9, we briefly looked at this passage in relation to its conclusion: that Agape Love is the greatest thing.

Of course, that conclusion was reached due to the content of the previous few verses. So, let's take a look:

'Love is patient, love is kind. It does not envy, it does not boast, it is not proud. It does not dishonour others, it is not self-seeking, it is not easily angered, it keeps no record of wrongs. Love does not delight in evil but rejoices with the truth. It always protects, always trusts, always hopes, always perseveres. Love never fails.' 1 Corinthians 13:4-8 NIV

What we have here is a detailed examination of the nature of Agape Love. It's like Paul dissects the DNA of Agape and exposes it for us all to see.

HAVE A GO

Now let's repeat the exercise we did earlier, but this time using 1 Corinthians 13. Read verses 4-8 out loud.

Then read the verses aloud again but this time using the word 'Agape' instead of Love, pausing after each phrase to briefly contemplate.

Notice again how both the passage and our understanding of Agape take on a new dimension.

These verses clearly show how Agape manifests. They demonstrate what characteristics should be evident in a life, if Agape is in operation.

By the way, if you take these characteristics of Agape in 1 Corinthians 13 and compare them to those revealed by God when He passed by before Moses on the mountain (see Song Chapter 29), you will notice striking similarities. [61]

That means of course that Jesus, if He IS pure Agape, should exude these characteristics.

To decide this for yourself, you may need to read or re-read the gospels, and make note of the different encounters, actions and reactions of Jesus. My own conclusion having done this is that Jesus lived and demonstrated Agape to the utmost.

What a first lesson in Love. True Love.

Now onto the second lesson we need to learn…and this one is about us.

---

[61] No wonder, it's the same DNA!

31. HOW DEEP IS YOUR LOVE 1977

Now we understand what Love is and looks like, the second lesson we need to learn is - how can we be people of Love?

Sadly, the word *'Christian'* has bad connotations for some people. This is usually as a result of a bad church experience or an unfortunate encounter with someone professing to be a Christian.

In essence, a Christian is simply a Christ follower. It is being an imitator of Jesus. It is not a religion. It is not a set of rules. It means to be a person of Agape. So, if I profess to be a Christian, the goal in all encounters with others, no matter who they are, should be to convey a Christlikeness in conversation, attitude and response − which is Agape.

That may be our goal… but how do we achieve it?

Let's return again to Song Chapter 11 and the second of the two questions I left you to ponder. Let's remind ourselves. It went something like this:

The Bible states that we as humans are made in the image and likeness of God. [62] *So, If God is Love and I am made in the image of God then can we conclude that I am Love, and can we say*

---

[62] Genesis 1:26-27

that if I want to know what Love is, I can look in the mirror?

Well, whereas for the first question we responded with a resounding *'yes'* about Jesus being a representation of Agape, I imagine the responses to this one may range from anything from woeful sighs to loud guffaws as we contemplate the sheer absurdity of the suggestion.

Yet…

In the beginning we *were* created in the image of God and according to the creation account in Genesis, God acknowledged the finished article as 'very good.' [63]

That indicates initially we were who we were meant to be - all unique beings reflecting God with the divine DNA within us.

This is important because I really believe at a deep core level of every human being *is* a foundation of Agape love, which begs the question, why then does it seem we are a million miles away from actually producing or living a life of Agape?

Remember our conclusions back in Song Chapter 25 (Love is a Battlefield) where we looked at how

---

[63] Genesis 1:31

the Eros nature has permeated society, and infiltrated our human beings?

We concluded we are all deeply infected by Eros - the self-centred 'I' disease that the Bible calls sin. Have another look at the Eros summary in Chapter 25 to refresh your memory.

The result of this Eros infection (which helps us to answer the above question) is that we have created what is a largely false persona based on our egos.

Fuelled by the Eros world all around us, we are conditioned as to what we're supposed to look like, be like, act like, what success is, what is valuable, what we need to aim for in life, what beauty is and what it means to love.

So, we have built and fashioned an image based on these values that our Eros saturated society bombard us with everywhere we turn. Then we spend most of our time catering to, protecting, defending, building and growing this self-image.

As a result, we will embrace and 'love' anything (e.g. status, reputation, material wealth) that feeds our self-image and look to eradicate all that opposes it.

As a result, those hooked arrows are everywhere.

The weird and disturbing thing is that all this builds a false 'you'. It is not the real 'you' at all. It's not who you were created to be. That's why a life lived building this 'false you' will only ever be an existence of shallowness (holistically), because it is outside of who you were designed to be and therefore outside of reality, outside of life, and outside of Agape. [64]

So, we're back to the question of 'how can we overcome this? How can we revert to the real me - and how can we develop Agape in our Eros saturated society?

One thing is for sure. It's not by trying harder and self-effort. I've tried that and it doesn't work! I'm sure some of you have too. We all know that pathway is doomed to failure.

We acknowledged earlier that we need help from an outside source. We need something to help us

---

[64] Thomas Merton in his book 'The Seeds of Contemplation" (New Directions 1949) argues that the high levels of insecurity and anxiety that exist within many people today is because... "...'the false self' is so fragile. It's inherently insecure because it's almost entirely a creation of the mind, a social construct. It doesn't exist except in the world of perception - instead of in God's Eternal Now."

transform radically. It feels like we need an Agape injection deep within us. Is that possible?

The answer is *'Yes'* and it's possible through the Holy Spirit.

Look at this verse in *Romans 5:5:*

'...the **Love of God** *has been poured out into our hearts by the Holy Spirit given to us.'* NKJV

The Holy Spirit is sometimes referred to as the third person of the Trinity. The Trinity is a foundational belief within the mainstream Christian faith that there is one God, but that one God exists in three persons: God the Father, God the Son, God the Holy Spirit.

This doctrine can take a bit of getting your head around.

Maths was never my forté at school, but even I knew 1+1+1 does not equal 1.

How can God be one yet three?

32. DANCE ME TO THE END OF LOVE 1984

To help us grasp this and to get where we're going, let's challenge a traditional mindset that exists about God.

I wouldn't say that my view of God was ever quite the stereotypical, old, wise man with a long white beard on a cloud. However, I guess for a big part of my life, I've still had this foundational concept of one supreme being as an all-powerful individual on a throne somewhere else.

In fact, probably most people, when the thought of 'God' enters their perception, would have a variation on that concept enter their minds. God up there in heaven looking down, with us down here looking up. We down here, are trying to get His attention up there with our prayers, hoping He up there will hear them and intervene down here, from time to time. [65]

(That may be a little exaggerated, but you get the concept).

---

[65] It's clear that some of the Biblical writers also had this concept. For example, check out David's writing in the Psalms e.g. Psalm 9, 11, 20. Of course, the Biblical writers were no different to us in that they were trying to understand and make sense of God in the midst of the culture of their world at that time.

It is only relatively recently (over the last decade or so) that a gradual paradigm shift has occurred in my thinking, which has led me to view God in a totally different way. This is how it happened.

It started when I discovered that the early Church Fathers had a Greek word that they used to describe the person of God as a triune (three-part) being.

The word was 'Perichoresis'

This is a compound word made up from two Greek words: **Peri** (meaning 'around' or 'circle') and **Choresis** (meaning 'dance' or 'flow').[66] So literally a 'circle dance'.

I became aware of a quite different perception of God from the more commonly held traditional view. God was not a static being but an ongoing movement – a 'circular flow', a kind of centrifugal force, with each person of the trinity encircling and enveloping the others in Love.

---

[66] This is the word where 'choreography' comes from.

This is a difficult concept to grasp initially, but I realised not an uncommon one. Many well known people of faith shared this thinking. For example C.S. Lewis [67] in his classic book 'Mere Christianity' describes God as a:

'dynamic, pulsating activity, an ever-present life force, a kind of drama, a kind of dance'.

I found myself starting to question my own perception of God. I realised that my own thinking on God was very jumbled. I believed Him to be close yet still in my mind, I defaulted to this image of this supreme being, operating in some kind of distant divine control room. And then the Trinity I saw as three very separate entities, responsible for different roles, and each doing their own thing in the big eternal plan.

But the idea of this triune God as a constant flowing force, in perfect harmony and communion with each other, made so much more sense. [68]

But then on top of this came the Agape revelation:

---

[67] C.S Lewis is the author of the Narnia books and was friends with J.R.R. Tolkien. Mere Christianity (First published 1952 in UK by Geoffrey Bles) has become a 'Christian Classic.'

[68] An author who has greatly inspired me and helped me in this is the wonderful Richard Rohr. Check out the fantastic *'The Divine Dance'(SPCK 2016)*...oh yes and all his other books.

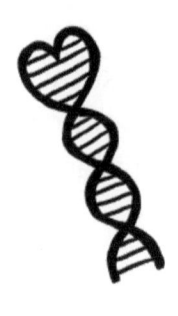

GOD the Father is Agape.

JESUS the Son is Agape (the exact representation of the father)

THE HOLY SPIRIT is Agape (simply the Spirit of God or Spirit of Agape)

So here's where I kind of arrived at in my thinking: At the centre of all existance and reality is this life force of Love, with the DNA of Agape flowing to and from each member of the trinity in perfect communion and relational harmony.

As we have heard, this has been likened to a dance. Can I now put in your minds another picture.

That of a Song.

A Love Song.

The Ultimate LoveSong!

So for a moment, think of this never ending song of Love sourced out of this interactive energy flow from God, which forms the very fabric of the universe.

This song of Agape, has the most beautiful harmony, the most glorious melody and the most splendiferous [69] rhythm pattern, transmitting from its divine source and then flowing outwards resonating through every aspect of creation, filling all in all, [70] holding all things together, sustaining life, always existing, always present, always working, always communicating, behind every vital impulse, every creative momentum, the ultimate reality of existance…

(That is worth one 'selah')

…but then poured into every individual heart that is open to receive!

(and that is worth a second one.)

I love how author Miroslav Volf puts it:

'*Because the Christian God is not a solo God, but rather a communion of three persons, faith leads human beings into the divine communion.*' [71]

That means you and I - we - are invited to join in and sing the song!

---

[69] Is that a word? If not, it should be!
[70] Ephesians 1:22-23/Colossians 3:11 NKJV
[71] Miroslav Volf, *After Our Likeness: The Church as the Image of the Trinity* (1998 Wm. B. Eerdmans Publishing Company)

33. LET YOUR LOVE FLOW 1976

God is very generous with the Holy Spirit.

Jesus himself said words to that effect: *'If earthly Dads know how to give good gifts to their kids, how much more will the heavenly Dad give the Holy Spirit to those that ask?'*[72]

This makes perfect sense. If Agape is the song that He wants us to sing, then He's obviously going to want to teach and equip us to sing the song, and what better way than to impart the very song itself; because of course to receive the Holy Spirit is to receive the very DNA of God.

But hang on. Let's get this right.

Are we saying this means the living God actually lives in anybody that invites Him in?
I mean that's crazy, isn't it?
A little hard to fathom perhaps?
And a little hard to believe?

The answer is Yes, Yes, Yes and Yes!

But it's true.

And this is why Paul gets so excited in his letter to

---

[72] Matthew 7:8-10 paraphrased

the Colossians where he talks about a great mystery, a plan that God has had all along, but that has been kept a secret through time.

Until now.

So, what is this great mystery that has now revealed?

*'This mystery has been kept in the dark for a long time, but now it's out in the open. God wanted everyone, not just Jews, to know this rich and glorious secret inside and out, regardless of their background, regardless of their religious standing. The mystery in a nutshell is just this: **Christ is in you.**'*[73]

There it is. <u>Christ is in you.</u>

If Christ really is in us, then that means that God is very close – He is with us all the time. **Always.**

Always close.

Always with us.

It also means Agape is always within,

which is the image of God,

which is the plan all along.

As author Peter J Leithart puts it: *"The Triune God*

---

[73] Colossians 1:27 TM

is in the world, nearer to us than we are to ourselves" and then he uses the phrase *"caught up into Communion."*[74]

Which is interesting, because Communion is the ritual in church life that is a central practice of the Christian faith, of taking bread and wine to represent the body and blood of Jesus. This is then consumed by the congregation.

I can forgive anyone who is not involved in church who thinks this ritual to be weird and even gruesome, but if we understand the picture of *His* body and blood being digested and becoming part of *our* body and blood; that is a very powerful reminder that He now lives within us, and we are as one with Him.

That really is Communion.

But then Leithart adds that this practice should result in us

"...being opened up so that other people may have room in us and we in them."

A kind of extended Communion?

We can think of this in two ways, both of which

---

[74] Peter J. Leithart, Traces of the Trinity: Signs of God in Creation and Human Experience. (2015 Baker Publishing Group)

enlarge our thinking.

The **first** application is to physical Communion in partaking in the sharing of the bread and wine.

This is beautifully described by Donald Nicholl in 'The Testing of Hearts' [75]

"The Eucharist [76] is a cosmic act, an act by which the redemptive love of Jesus permeates the whole cosmos... receiving communion is not merely for the good of an individual or even a particular ecclesiastical group, but is participation in a cosmic act which benefits all creation.'

He then goes on to say:

"Therefore, in receiving communion, one is a representative of all creation, and so if one is in a position to receive communion while one's friends are for some reason excluded, then apart from anything else, it is an act of friendship to partake on their behalf"

What an enlarging thought, and what an example of *'opening up to make room for others'* using the terminology of Leithart.

---

[75] Donald Nicholl 'The Testing of the Hearts' (New edition 1998 Darton Longman and Todd Ltd). A powerful book and a must read.
[76] Another name for Communion. It is a Greek word that compounded means 'The Good Gift'

The **second** application is to the spiritual communion of 'Christ in You'. Receiving Agape from Him is not just so we can sit back and bask in the wonder of God's Love, but that just as the song is now part of us, we do all we can to enable others to hear it.'

If we continue reading into the next verse of the Colossians 1 passage, we just looked at:

'*The mystery in a nutshell is just this: Christ is in you, so therefore you can look forward to sharing in God's glory. It's that simple*'. [77]

We are able to share in God's glory, His nature. How? We now have the DNA within us.

John puts it as simply as this - '*we are able to love* (Agape) *because He first loved* (Agape) *us*'. [78]

The Love must keep flowing!

In us, through us, from us, between us.

---

[77] Colossians 1|:27,28 TM

[78] the explanation from John following His teaching that God is Agape in 1 John 4:19

There's a wonderful natural feature in the holy land that provides us with a great spiritual lesson. It involves the river that runs down the backbone of the Holy Land, the River Jordan. It starts from Mt Hermon high up in the North and runs southward gradually descending for some 250 km.

On its journey, it flows into 2 main bodies of water; Lake Galilee and the Dead Sea.

The contrast between these two bodies of water is extraordinary. Galilee is fresh, alive, full of fish and surrounded by a lush, green landscape, whereas the Dead Sea is barren, fishless and lifeless. The only thing that lives in the Dead Sea are tourists floating in the buoyancy created by the high salt content.

Why is that? It's the same water from the same river flowing in.

The answer is with the Dead Sea there is no outflow.

At Galilee there in an inflow <u>and</u> an outflow maintaining movement freshness and life. The only exit for the water at the Dead Sea is evaporation. Where there is no outflow, things become

…DEAD

In the wonderful book 'Tuesdays with Morrie' by Mitch Albom, [79] a dying professor shares life lessons with a former student. On one encounter comes this gem:

'The most important thing in life is to learn how to give out love and to let it come in as well'

I'm convinced that's what Jesus was trying to explain in the encounter he had with a woman at a well, recorded in the gospel account of John.

He proclaims himself as the source of living water which when received becomes *'like a flowing fountain that gives eternal life.'* [80]

I think that is God's purpose for you whoever you are, along with every human being, to come to the source of Agape, drink deep, get filled and then allow that Love to flow out of you.

And believe it or not, that's the way this world will ultimately be transformed according to Jesus:

---

[79] If you haven't read *'Tuesdays with Morrie'* (1997 Doubleday), please do. It is a truly wonderful, joy filled, tearful, soul enlarging read!

[80] John 4:14 CEV

*By this everyone **will know** that you are my disciples, if you Love (Agape) one another.* [81]

Let's just run over that again to make sure we grasp this. What is it that will reveal a person or people to be Christ's disciples according to Jesus?

Church services?

Evangelistic programmes?

Prayer?

No – as important as they may be – ultimately, it's through an Agape revolution! When our image reflects His image!

Julian, who was Roman Emperor from 355-363, hated Christians. In fact, he attempted a pagan revival following the increasing popularity of the Jesus Movement. But within his annuls, he reluctantly admits:

'Nothing has contributed to the progress of the superstition of the Christians as their charity (an old-fashioned word for Love) to strangers...the impious Galileans provide not only for their own

---

[81] John 13:35 NIV

poor but for ours as well.'[82]

When we have the flow operating, there is life and blessing and health and goodness and joy. It may not be welcomed by everyone. In fact, it is likely to stir up Eros in strange ways (like Julian above).

But when Love outflows as it should, the Song will be heard and for many it truly becomes not only irresistible but also transformational.

Paul summarises it beautifully in his first letter to the Thessalonians: *"May the Lord make your love increase and overflow for each other and for everyone else, just as ours does for you."*[83]

As we come to the end of this section of the book, let us summarise the two vital lessons we set out to learn.

Lesson 1 which we learnt in Song Chapters 29 and 30 was how to recognise **what Agape looked like.**

Lesson 2 which we have learnt in Song Chapters 31, 32 and 33 was **how we can begin to be a person of Agape.**

---

[82] Sozom 5:16 - This is from the 5th of 9 books on Church History by Sozomen in the AD 300's, each book accounting for life during the reign of a different Roman Emperor.
[83] 1 Thessalonians 3:12, NIV

Now before we move on to the finale, just one last thing which is important to bear in mind.

34. YOU CAN'T HURRY LOVE 1982

In the New Testament you will come across passages that talk about both gifts of the Spirit [84] (examples include prophecy, teaching, leadership and giving) and fruit of the Spirit [85] (examples include joy, peace, gentleness and kindness).

The source of both gifts and fruit is the same: The Holy Spirit.

The recipient of both gifts and fruit are the same: normal men and women like you and I who carry the DNA of God via the Holy Spirit.

However, there is a major difference.

Gifts are given. Fruit is grown.

Gifts are all about **what we do** and are given by God to enable us to be effective in daily life. Fruit is about **who we are** – it's about being and becoming!

Now, if you look at the list of the fruits of the Spirit in Galatians 5, guess which is the first on the list?

---

[84] Romans 12 and 1 Corinthians 12 are 2 chapters which give examples of spiritual gifts.
[85] Galatians 5 contains a list of 9 fruits in verses 22 and 23.

Love. Agape.

Love is a **fruit** of the Spirit.

It would be nice if it were a gift, but there's no such thing as 'instant' love.

Agape is the result of a journey through life, growing, learning, understanding, experiencing, (Oh …and messing up!)

That's why we must be committed to the long haul.

A young fruit tree starts with a few branches bearing fruit, but give that tree 20 to 30 years and, unless there's a disease that takes hold, the output can be stunning and many people will be able to be nourished and fed from its fruit.

So as a word of encouragement, if you get frustrated by your Agape output, hang on in there.

Jesus uses a word picture in John Chapter 15 of a vine with branches. He himself is the vine. His followers are the branches.

It is the branches that bear fruit, but in doing so, each branch is totally reliant on the life of the vine to flow into it.

So, the message is very simple: stay connected to the vine and Agape fruit will happen!

You don't have to try and make this happen. [When did you last pass an apple tree and hear a branch groaning 'I must try harder, I must do better…'?].

The branch need do nothing other than make sure it stays connected to its life source.

So don't expect to be an Agape Grandmaster within the first few months.

Start small with the basics.

Take it day by day and celebrate when you recognise the straight arrows that appear (sometimes surprisingly) from you.

Of course, bearing fruit involves a practice known as 'waiting'.

I have discovered 'waiting' has one common denominator to all human beings - Everyone dislikes it intensely.

Let's face it, standing in a queue at the supermarket checkout, being stuck a traffic jam or sitting in a hospital waiting room are never going to rank as our favourite moments. I can honestly confess I have never woken up at the start of a day and thought 'I hope I'm in for a good spot of waiting today!' Have you?

Over the last few decades, modern appliances, cashpoint machines, instant meals, on demand TV, social media, internet streaming and online shopping (with next day delivery) are a few of the things that have led to a consumer society which now expects and even demands instant service and results.

Consequently, waiting is viewed as a major inconvenience.

Yet most things of God are not instant. It takes time for a bud on a tree to become ripe fruit. There's a process needed and this process is going on all the time.

Yet you can't actually see it. If you got a chair and sat by a fruit tree to watch the process, you wouldn't see anything. But if you visit the tree, say once a week, you may notice small gradual changes. But you can't hurry the process. You just have to wait until the process is complete and the fruit has ripened.

The same principles apply with spiritual fruit, including

Agape Love. Truth be told, there are no short cuts in the area of character development.

Now if this all seems a bit daunting, don't worry, there's some good news: *Patience* is a fruit of the Spirit too. Isn't God good!

(In fact, all accompanying fruits help in producing of Agape.) [86]

So, remember: *'You can't hurry Love, you've just got to wait.'*

---

[86] I once heard it taught a long time ago (source well forgotten) that in the list of fruit in Galatians 5, that in the original language, it could be read as if there was a colon (i.e. punctuation mark) after 'Agape'. In other words, the fruit of the Spirit is Love: joy, peace patience etc...which then can be read: 'The fruit of the Spirit is Agape <u>out of which flows</u> joy, peace, patience etc... I can't verify this, but I like it!

FINALE

I'll make the time if you name the day. Trouble or shine
I love you anyway
I think of you as child of clay. Whatever you do...

... I love you anyway

'Love Anyway' by Mike Scott. [c/f footnote 99]`

35. CAN YOU FEEL THE LOVE TONIGHT? 1994

"The earth is filled with your love, Lord..." Psalm 119:64 NIV

What a beautiful declaration.

I like to think of this being in many ways God's 'mission statement' and His heart and goal for this world we inhabit.

As we read the daily papers or watch the news bulletins however, the thought of this being a reality may seem a million miles away.

In a sense it probably is. Yet in another maybe it isn't.

You see maybe it's already happening. Maybe the earth is already filled with His Love.

Let's go back to the word picture we introduced back in Song Chapter 32 where we started to challenge the stereotype image of God as a static being, in favour of a dynamic interactive energy flow with God as a Trinitarian being.

We viewed God at the centre of all existence, emitting this never-ending LoveSong, which resounds through the whole created universe.

It's a song of the Father, a song of the Creator, a song of the Saviour, a song of the Spirit, a song of a Lover, a song of Agape.

I want to suggest to you that this one giant LoveSong is already being sung and what is happening is simply that more and more people are discovering the song, hearing it, learning its melody and starting to join in.

My question to you is '<u>Do **you** recognise the Song</u>? Do you Hear it? Do you Sense it? Can you Feel it?

To which some of you will undoubtedly say, "Well I'd like to, but I simply don't!"

If that is your response, I fully understand that, because I too watch the news and 'yes' I know this world is a mess. I know there's injustice beyond reason, I know there are global pandemics, I know man continues to damage the planet, I know the constant negative propaganda we get bombarded with from the media, I know the internet can be destructively evil, I know about wars and famines, drug trafficking and prejudice and exploitation, etc.

But there's a sound, a Song that is rising in the midst of all these things.

In an Eros fuelled world, the Agape Song can be heard and it's getting louder. It is growing and more ears are being attuned to it, more voices are adding to it, more harmonies are developing it, more instruments are helping build it.

And so, let me ask again: Do you hear the LoveSong?

If not, let me in this finale section, try and adjust your 'pitch', so you too can hear the Song.

The first thing to understand is that despite anything and everything, the Song resounds because we – you and I, are already loved.

The straight arrow of Agape has already been fired, and the exciting truth is that nothing or no one can change that.

Which in turn means nothing can change this:

God is Love
And
God Loves You!

36. I WILL ALWAYS LOVE YOU 1992

My own personal favourite chapter in the whole Bible is Romans 8 which concludes with these words!

For I am convinced that neither death nor life, neither angels nor demons, neither the present nor the future, nor any powers, neither height nor depth, nor anything else in all creation, will be able to separate us from the love of God that is in Christ Jesus our Lord."[87] NIV

Oh, come on, lets 'selah' that!

You have been Loved, you are Loved and you will be Loved and NOTHING can separate you from that Love. Death can't. Demons can't! Powers can't, and you can't. Even if you are reading this and you don't want to be Loved. Sorry, but you are!

That's why the concept of 'hell' as a place of eternal separation from God for 'bad' or 'unforgiven' people is worth questioning. [88]

---

[87] Romans 8:38-39 NIV. These are the stunning last verses to an already stunning chapter.

[88] Never be afraid to question doctrines and teachings, even mainstream thinking that you've always been taught. This is not a sign of weakness of faith but of strength. It shows you are secure enough to allow the structure of your faith to be prodded and poked.

I know that will be uncomfortably challenging to some readers, but think about it, Paul doesn't say 'there's nothing that can separate us from God's Agape…except hell.' [If that was the case, hell would be more powerful than Agape! Can you imagine 1 Corinthians 13 finishing 'and the greatest of all…is hell?]

Let's read it one more time from a different version:

'*I am **sure** that **nothing** can separate us from God's Love - not life or death, not angels or spirits, not the present or the future, and not powers above or powers below. **Nothing** in all creation can separate us from God's Love for us in Christ Jesus our Lord!*' CEV

Note that Paul is not 50:50 about this, he's *convinced, certain, **sure**.*

And I am too!

The word 'Gospel' as has already been said, means *good news*. One of the key reasons it is such *good news* is because God's Love for you is not reliant on your response.

It can't be, otherwise it's not Agape.

This is the best news ever.

So often, the traditional message recognised as the 'gospel' seems to have shrunk down to how we can individually be saved from our awfulness. Linked in with this, is the belief that if an individual doesn't respond positively to the message and doesn't pray the right prayer - well, as Private Frazer would say in the classic 70's BBC Sitcom 'Dad's Army':

"we're all Dooomed"

I don't know about you, but the thought of the vast majority of human history being condemned to a godless eternity doesn't seem much of a 'gospel' to me. It may be good news for a tiny minority of the population - those who respond and say the 'sinner's prayer' - but for the rest who don't, which is most of the people who have ever lived - its terrible news.

For me that's a ('love'?) song I just can't join in with anymore.

Despite all this and whether or not you agree or disagree with me, the reality of this message of good news is SO MUCH BIGGER than just getting an individual to pray the 'sinner's prayer'.

I believe the Song of the true gospel proclaims a cosmic hope for history, for the planet, and for the whole of society.

It's a Song that goes out to the lost, lonely, bound, broken hearted, those who are in the darkest places wanting to escape, and those in the darkest places who don't.

It's a Song which will continue to be sung for every living creature, because there is no being who is outside the love and mercy of Agape.

It's a Song that extends out to the extremities of existence and going back to that phenomenal prayer in Ephesians 3, (c/f Footnote 21), Paul shows his deep desire for the reader to try and comprehend this vastness:

'...that you, being rooted and grounded in Love (Agape), may be able to comprehend with all the saints what is the width, and length and depth and height - to know the Love (Agape) of Christ which passes all knowledge, that you may be filled with all the fullness of God' (verses 17-19 NKJV).

Note:

Width	– that it is <u>all</u> Inclusive.
Breadth	– that it is <u>all</u> Encompassing.
Depth	– that it is <u>all</u> Sufficient.
Height	– that it is <u>all</u> Supreme

Out of this unfathomable love, God is restoring and healing everything.

The whole thing is being put back together, and each of us are invited to be a part of this gigantic restoration project.

Yes, **this** is the Song we are called to sing and the simple message is "This a Song you must hear. It is the most beautiful sound. Listen to it, hear it – learn it and then come to the gig – join in with the crowd, and as we allow the words, the melody, the rhythm, and the harmony to flow, then together, as one voice, we raise an anthem of True Love".

And such are the vast extremities of this Love, then absolutely **everyone** is invited to join in and sing.

This song will continue to be sung when everything else vanishes.

37. WHOLE LOTTA LOVE 1969

You will find this invitation to sing this Song echoing throughout the pages of the whole Bible. Right from when God started to gather a people in the days of Moses, [89] through the Old Testament Judges, [90] the Kings, [91] the Prophets [92] and then into the New Testament, [93] through to the very final book in the Bible, Revelation. [94]

But the place you'll most frequently come across it is in the Psalms.

The book of Psalms is the longest book in the Bible - a collection of 150 songs, hymns and musical prayers found in the Old Testament and written by a variety of authors including David, Solomon and Moses.

---

[89] Exodus 15:1
[90] Judges 5:3,12
[91] 2 Chronicles 20:22
[92] Isaiah 42:10-12
[93] Colossians 3:16
[94] Revelation 15:3

HAVE A GO

Here's a quick fun little exercise to have a go at. If you pick up a closed Bible and then look at the page edges of the closed pages - try and guess the half way point and then open it at that point. Hopefully you've found Psalms.

(If not, the likelihood is you either hit Job, in which case you've gone too short, OR you hit Proverbs, and you've gone too long.

If you hit Revelation, ring the Doctor!)

It somehow seems fitting that this songbook has been placed in a central location within the structure of the Bible. It's a book that's often very central to the lives of its readers, commonly cited as a favourite.

I'm sure that one of the reasons for this is, that this collection of songs involves real people doing real life in raw, honest communication with God.

If you start to read them, one thing you will soon notice is that the writers certainly don't hold back. They outpour their thoughts and feelings with no holds barred, both in the good celebratory times (such as times of victory, answered prayer, healing and blessing) and the dark times (confronting fear, loss, doubt, worry, failure, danger, disappointment and sickness).

It's fair to say that within the collection of 150 Psalms, you'll find one for just about every scenario that life delivers. (Not surprisingly, there is no shortage of Eros on display too.)

That is why so many people over the centuries have found that they can connect with this book so well. It is like the words of these ancient poems and songs penned so long ago, somehow become ours in the right now. We find we can relate to the situations and accompanying emotions that the writers experienced in the past, and this in turn can help us express to God how we're feeling in the present.

Yet through all the different seasons of life portrayed throughout the Psalms, there remains an almost separate Song, that keeps emerging time and time again:

The LoveSong.

'I will sing of the Lord's great Love forever' declares the opening verse of Psalm 89 '...*to all generations*' NIV and is just one of many refrains of the song.

Not only is this LoveSong regularly on show but the invitation to join in runs parallel too.

Check out the following Psalms for some examples: 34:3, 81:1, 95:1, 100:1, 117:1.

38. EVERYTHING IS LOVE 2018

But it's not only mankind that is called to sing.

All of creation is invited to join in.

This massive, sweeping appeal continues to re-occur through the book of Psalms, and then just as we are nearing the end, it all seems to come together in one gigantic, all-encompassing ensemble in Psalm 148.

The Psalm naturally seems to divide into two halves.

The first half focuses on the heavens: this includes the 'seen' realm - sun, moon, stars, planets, atmosphere - they're invited to sing [95] as well as the 'unseen' realms - the angels and the heavenly hosts.

Then the second half of Psalm 148 involves everything on the earth - sea creatures, elements, seasons, mountains, hills, trees, animals, insects, birds. They are all invited too.

---

[95] Did you know the stars sing? I'm not talking famous people here but literally astronomical objects. A few years ago, astronomers whilst researching stars caught an ancient cluster emitting a sound that can only be described as a musical arrangement. You can search this online and find lots of clips of this, but one good article with succinct explanation and examples is in a 'Wired' online article: the link is-
https://www.wired.co.uk/article/astronomers-ancient-stars-singing-milky-way

Two Psalms later, the book ends with Psalm 150, a relatively short six verse conclusion to the whole book, which is a call for more voices and instruments to add to the sound, melody and rhythm of the Song.

The last verse of this last Psalm has this bold and simple invitation:

'Everything that has breath praise the Lord' NKJV

Heaven and Earth

Men and Angels

Seen and Unseen

Everything and Everyone

An invitation to join in with one massive, universal Song!

39. WHEN LOVE TAKES OVER 2009

Let us draw this all together by understanding God's ultimate will, plan and goal.

It is a simple plan, which runs right through Scripture and it's this:

There will one day be a day.

A day we are moving towards and we are closer to that day today than we were yesterday.

On this day – Love will take over!

The more I've read and studied the Bible over the years the more this big picture comes into view. You start to see God's plan unfolding over time.

Way back in Genesis 12, God reveals to a man called Abraham, this idea of a group of people, a family, a nation through which <u>all people everywhere</u> will be blessed. From that point on, there begins the formation of this family through the bloodline of 'Father' Abraham.

By the time we get to Exodus, Abraham's grandson Jacob, has had 12 sons and it is they who become the foundational named 12 tribes of this nation called Israel.[96]

The important thing to remember is God's purpose for gathering this family/nation is never to make an exclusive club, but ultimately to bless one and all, everybody, everywhere.

When we read the New Testament, we see that Old Testament Israel, is a foreshadowing of the church[97] called to share this wonderful gospel message of Love, salvation and inclusiveness brought about through Jesus, that life is available for everyone through an Agape revolution.

But of course, right here is one of the problems.

The church has through history largely failed to live up to this calling. As we concluded in our earlier 'arrow spotting exercises', this God ordained structure that was created to reflect Agape, has itself become Eros-infected. Today, our communities are not short of people who once belonged to a local

---

[96] By the way, if you've ever wondered why there are long and seemingly tedious genealogies at certain points in scripture, the reason is to carefully outline this family tree. The exciting thing is when we hit the New Testament, we see the purpose for both gospel genealogies in Matthew (Chapter 1:1-16) and Luke (Chapter 3:23-38), which is to show that Jesus emerges from the same bloodline.

[97] 1 Peter 2:9, Ephesians 2:19-20

church, but no longer attend due to some incident that has left them feeling either hurt, betrayed, wounded, or embittered.

From the many people I have encountered over the years that find themselves in this situation, my conclusion is that most are not anti-God. In fact, many still have a strong faith, pray and trust in Jesus.

They have simply lost all respect and belief in 'the Church.'

What is the answer and what can we do about this? The answer is we need to understand and communicate a vital distinction!

The distinction is this:

Love (Agape) never fails. People always will.

This is a vital foundational mind-set that needs to be adopted, because the church is always about people. It is not a building. 'Church' is a term from its Greek origins that simply means a gathering together of people.

There is a false supposition which exists that somehow if you are one of those people that gather (in other words, a 'church goer'), that you've somehow got it all together and have no problems.

That false notion over the years has created untold damage. It has resulted in people assuming unrealistic expectations and then wearing 'masks'; putting on a show of 'holiness' and pretending they have it all together, because that is what they think is expected. This in turn has created a false facade, an existence of unreality and a hypocrisy that can be smelt a mile away.

This has also had a negative impact on many people who have had no previous experience of church, but tentatively start to make enquiries wondering if the church can help them.

Maybe they are seeking answers, spiritual direction or help with a particular problem. But the outcome on far too many occasions has not been a discovery of Agape inclusiveness but either:

The discovery of a culture that is totally foreign and irrelevant to where they are at.

OR

The discovery of a set of religious rules that are expected to be upheld, setting forth moral standards that are both overwhelming and impossible to live up to.

OR

The discovery of a wall built between those who are *'in'* the church and those who are *'not in'* the church, with those *'in'* trying to get those *'not in'* to come *'in'* through as many imaginative Eros hooks as can be mustered.

All these discoveries almost always have the same result: people stay away, and in some cases make a decision the church is not and will never be for them. The saddest thing is when 'God', 'Jesus' and anything spiritual is included in the decision as a package.

Please understand I am not anti-church. I love the church, and when it functions with an Agape foundation, there is nothing else like it on earth.

But there are no perfect churches. The truth is all people, church attenders or not, fall short and fail.

It's been said *'If you happen to find a perfect church, don't go there, because you'll mess it up',* and that's the whole point.

The 'real' church is simply an assembly of people who are fully aware of their failings, but also fully aware that at the centre of it all is the one who came to love and restore people who have failings.

They are a group of people who acknowledge their imperfect nature, but they also acknowledge that there is a perfect one who invites them to come to Him, receives them as they are and loves them, whoever they are and offers hope for change.

An authentic church is one that gathers, having heard and become enthralled by the transforming beauty of the LoveSong, compelled to explore its depths, to learn its rhythm and melodies and to sing the words of unfailing love that is for all people, everywhere.

The beauty of the true church is that at its centre is the person of Jesus Christ – the Love that never fails.

Who could refuse that?

But you see that is why the distinction is necessary, because until unfailing Love becomes all in all – everything in everyone, everywhere – then disappointments, hurts, betrayals, and failures will continue to exist in our world, both inside and outside the church.

But let's remind ourselves of the statement made earlier:

There will come a day.

A day when Love will take over…

On this day, every aspect of creation, past present and future

Every man, woman and child

Every creature on land, sea and air

Every feature of nature – trees, mountains, rocks, valleys

Every cosmic phenomenon, planets, stars, galaxies, solar systems

All earth and its inhabitants

All heaven along with its hosts of angels

Everything seen, unseen, temporary and eternal

<u>Everything will come together.</u>

All that is wrong will be put right.

The voice of Eros in whatever form it takes, will be silent.

Everything and everyone will be restored through the power of Agape! [98]

---

[98] I've compiled my Top ten 'full restoration' scriptures in Appendix A. Have a read through and 'Selah'.

Full complete restoration…

…<u>of EVERYTHING!</u>

Your Kingdom come, Your will be done, On earth as it is in heaven

I don't know about you, but there's something within me that longs for that one day.

But until it comes, what do we do?

I think we've kind of answered it already, but as a clarifying reminder, the answer I think, is nicely summarised in a short little verse in the book of Isaiah 44:23 which states:

'Tell the heavens and the earth to start singing! CEV

The implication is 'Why Wait?' Let's start singing this LoveSong right now!

40. LOVESONG 2011

> *'Open up your heart and sing your song right through me'*
> 'You in the Sky' Mike Scott & the Waterboys '[99]

I guess an obvious final question is why doesn't God wrap it all up now?

Answer? I don't really know!

What I do know is that our life purpose is to receive Agape and let it flow onwards to others. It's as simple as that! Well…in theory!

Sometimes I seem to do OK with this, other times not so. I am still aware I have so much Eros in me.

---

[99] Mike Scott is lead vocalist for the band The Waterboys. They've been one of my favourite bands since I saw them support U2 at Wembley back in the 80s and believe it or not, outshone them. Mike Scott is an interesting character, and has experimented with spirituality in many different directions. Yet some of his lyrics are as close to an Agape understanding as anyone else I've come across. [I've used some from one of my favourite songs 'Love Anyway' from the album 'Still Burning' at the start of each section of this book, [*with acknowledgement to Sony Music/ATV Ltd*] His autobiography is worth a read: *'Adventures of a Waterboy Remastered' (2017 Outline Press Ltd)'* My wife thinks I've read this more than once!

Yet I know I must continue to sing, even though I'm aware all the time it's a perfect Song from an imperfect singer!

I know God is in the hook straightening business, and I know he will continue to do that work in my life through His Spirit if I allow Him access.

I also have to remember that this imperfect singer is not called to demonstrate how I've got it all together, or how far advanced I am in the 'School of Holiness'.

Instead, I have to remind myself that this is all part of the song itself! I am Loved by God wherever I am at (warts and all) and I must love others wherever they are at (warts and all).

Somehow, that gives the Song another level of beauty!

Writers say the last words of a book are often the hardest to find. If that's the case I am very fortunate because about half way through writing this, I came across a quote that was so brilliant, there was never any other contender for the last words.

The quote is from the Russian novelist Dostoyevsky [100] and the reason it is so brilliant is that it is like a Love Song on its own, in so much that it encapsulates, far better than I ever could, what it means to sing the Song!

So over and out from me and I humbly hand over to Dostoyevsky for the last words:

*"**Love** people even in their sin, for that is the semblance of Divine **Love** and is the highest **Love** on earth. **Love** all of God's creation, the whole and every grain of sand of it. **Love** every leaf, every ray of God's light. **Love** the animals, **Love** the plants, **Love** everything. If you **Love** everything, you will perceive the divine mystery in things. Once you perceive it, you will begin to comprehend it better every day. And you will come at last to **Love** the whole world with an all-embracing **Love**."*

---

[100] Fyodor Dostoyevsky – The Brothers Karamazov (1879-80 The Russian Messenger). This author is best known for 'Crime and Punishment'. My wife is a big fan of Russian literature and has read Tolstoy's War and Peace and Anna Karenina several times. I have read none!

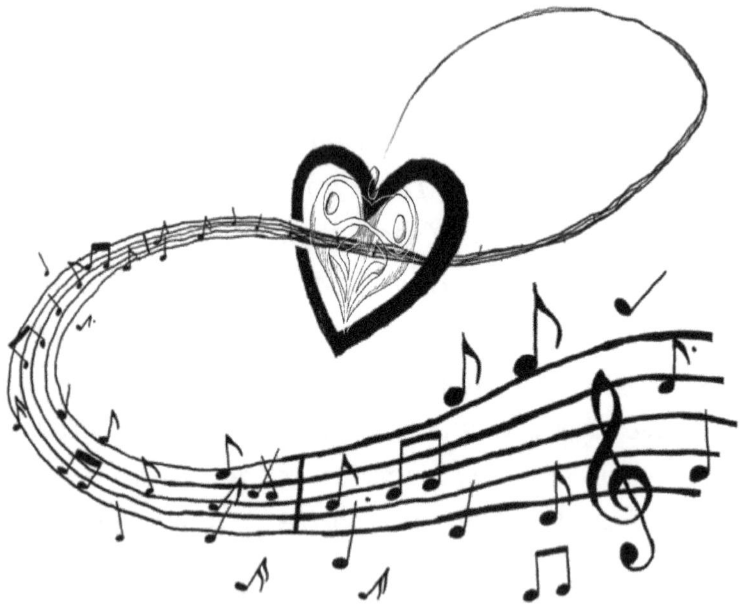

ENCORE

Whatever you do... I love you anyway
  'Love Anyway' by Mike Scott

Appendix A: My Top 10 'Full Restoration' verses

Appendix B: Bible Versions and Translations

Appendix C: Love Song Quiz Answers

Appendix D: Acknowledgements

Appendix A: My 'Top 10' New Testament 'Full Restoration' Verses

1. `God has now revealed to us His mysterious will regarding Christ - which is to fulfil His own good plan. And this is the plan: `At the right time <u>He will bring everything together</u> under the authority of Christ - <u>everything in heaven and on earth</u>.` Ephesians 1:9-10 NLT

2. `For God was pleased to have all his fullness dwell in Him, and through Him to <u>reconcile to Himself all things</u>, whether things on earth or things in heaven, by making peace through His blood, shed on the cross.` Colossians 1:19-20 NIV

3. `Yes, Adam's one sin brings condemnation <u>for everyone</u>, but Christ's one act of righteousness brings a right relationship with God and new life <u>for everyone</u>.` Romans 5:18 NLT

4. `We see Jesus, who was made a little lower than the angels for the suffering of death crowned with glory and honour that He by the grace of God might taste death <u>for Everyone</u>.` Hebrews 2:9 NKJV

5.`....all created beings in heaven and on earth—even those long ago dead and buried—will bow in worship before this Jesus Christ.` Philippians 2:10 TM

6. `He gave his life to purchase freedom for everyone. This is the message God gave to the world at just the right time.` 1 Timothy 2:6 NLT

7. `For the grace of God has been revealed, bringing salvation to all people.` Titus 2:11 NIV

8. `And they will not need to teach their neighbours, nor will they need to teach their relatives, saying, 'You should know the LORD.` For everyone, from the least to the greatest, will know me already.` Hebrews 8:11 NLT

9. `He is the reconciliation for our sins, and not for ours only, but also for the sins of the whole world.` I John 2:2 NKJV

10. `For the time being He must remain out of sight in heaven until everything is restored to order again.` Acts 3:21 TM

And one Old Testament verse from the Psalms for the road...

`..all flesh shall bless His holy name Forever and ever.` - Psalm 145:21 NKJV

Appendix B: Bible Translations and Versions

You'd think it would be a simple task to buy a Bible today. But the sheer volume of choices of different versions and translations can be overwhelming. How did there come to be so many, and what's the best or right one for me?

Before answering this, a brief bit of history.

The Old Testament text was originally written in ancient Hebrew and was passed down through the generations with scrupulous care by scribes who hand wrote copies from the original. From about the 6th Century AD a group known as *the Masoretes* became responsible for the preservation of the sacred scriptures. From this group the Ben Asher text emerged and in the 12th century was the only recognised form of Holy Scripture. Daniel Bomberg printed the first Hebrew Bible in 1516-17. The Septuagint (translation into Greek) and the Vulgate (translation into Latin) followed.

The New Testament text was written in Koine Greek and has more manuscript support than any other body of ancient literature with over 5,000 Greek and 8,000 Latin manuscripts. The 27 books that formulate the New Testament as we know it were canonised (first brought together) in 367 by Athanasius, Bishop of Alexandria, after years of deliberation. It is remarkable that aside from minor variations, there is an overwhelming agreement between all the ancient texts and only one basic New Testament exists.

The Bible as we know it today is believed to have been first assembled by St. Jerome around A.D. 400. This manuscript included all 39 books of the Old Testament and the 27 books of the New Testament in the same language: Latin. The first translation into English was in 1611 known as the Authorised Version or King James Bible (named such as the translation was commissioned by King James I)

Versions Today

As already stated, there are a vast number of versions available today. Which one should you choose? A summary below may help you through the maze.

In simplified terms, Bibles available to purchase can be put into one of three categories:

1. **LITERAL TRANSLATIONS** - this is where the translator will take the original text and translate it as close to the original language as possible. So

the King James Version (KJV) is still one of the most popular today along with the New American Standard Version (NASV).

2. THE DYNAMIC EQUIVELENTS – this is where the translator will take the original text and translate the words from the original language into their precise equivalent into today's language. A couple of the best and most popular examples would be the New International Version (NIV) or New Living Translation (NLT).

3. FREE – this is where the translator has less concern about exact words of the original text and seeks to impart the general idea or meaning behind it. Therefore, rather than an actual translation, it is more of a paraphrasing. Examples would be The Message (TM) and The Living Bible.

So, which is best? My answer is all of them! All are helpful and all have advantages and disadvantages.

One great solution is a parallel text Bible, where you can find 3 or 4 different translations side by side. These are available in hard copy or digitally online in any good Bible programme (e.g., Biblegateway.com or Biblehub.com).

One Christian author, who used a wide variety of different translations throughout his book, was once asked why he did not use just one version for the whole book instead of a different one for each example.

His answer was that he had to find the right translation that best fitted in with his doctrine!

An awesome answer…and a practice that over the years I unashamedly admit to putting into practice. However, on this occasion, I wanted to choose half a dozen popular versions that would give examples of the 3 categories above, which in turn would hopefully give you a feel of the way each is written.

The abbreviations for the different translations I have used and referred to in 'LoveSong' are:

CEV - Contemporary English Version

KJV - King James Version

NKJV - New King James Version

NIV - New International Version

NLT - New Living Translation

TM - The Message Translation

Appendix C: Love Song Quiz Answers

1 Point for each answer (4 points for Song 27)

1. *Love is in the Air* 1977 – JOHN PAUL YOUNG
2. *We Found Love* 2011 – RIHANNA ft CALVIN HARRIS
3. *Crazy Little Thing Called Love* 1979 – QUEEN
4. *Silly Love Songs* 1976 – WINGS
5. *Birds do It (Let's fall in Love)* 1928 – COLE PORTER
6. *LoveSong* 1989 – THE CURE
7. *All You Need is Love* 1967 – THE BEATLES
8. *Labelled with Love* 1981 – SQUEEZE
9. *Love is all Around* 1994 – WET WET WET
10. *What is Love?* 1984 – HOWARD JONES
11. *I Want to Know What Love is* 1987 – FOREIGNER
12. *Words of Love* 1957 – BUDDY HOLLY
13. *Lovesexy* 1988 – PRINCE
14. *You Give Love a Bad Name* 1986 – BON JOVI
15. *Scary Love* 2018 – THE NEIGHBOURHOOD

16. *You've Lost that Lovin' Feeling* 1964 - THE RIGHTEOUS BROTHERS

17. *Tainted Love* 1981 - SOFT CELL

18. *Higher Love* 1986 - STEVE WINWOOD

19. *The Look of Love* 1982 - ABC

20. *Love is an Arrow* 1985 - ABERFELDY

21. *The One I Love* 1987 - REM

22. *I will do Anything for Love* 1993 - MEAT LOAF

23. *I See Love Everywhere I Look* 2006 - MELYNNIQUE SEABROOKE

24. *This ain't no Love Song, this is Goodbye* 2010 - SCOUTING FOR GIRLS

25. *Love is a Battlefield* 1983 - PAT BENATAR

26. *Love Me Tender* 1957 - ELVIS PRESLEY

27. *The Power of Love* 1984/1985/1985/1994 - FRANKIE GOES TO HOLLYWOOD/ JENNIFER RUSH/ HUEY LEWIS & THE NEWS/ CELINE DION

28. *Stop! In the Name of Love* 1965 - DIANA ROSS & THE SUPREMES

29. *Lessons in Love* 1985 - LEVEL 42

30. *True Love* 2013 - PINK ft LILY ALLEN

31. *How deep is Your Love* 1977 - THE BEE GEES

32. *Dance Me to the End of Love* 1984 - LEONARD COHAN

33. *Let Your Love Flow* 1974 - THE BELLAMY BROTHERS

34. *You Can't Hurry Love* 1982 - PHIL COLLINS

35. *Can You Feel the Love Tonight?* 1994 - ELTON JOHN

36. *I will Always Love You* 1992 - WHITNEY HOUSTON

37. *Whole Lotta Love* 1969 - LED ZEPPELIN

38. *Everything is Love* 2018 - BEYONCE & JAY-Z

39. *When Love Takes Over* 2009 - DAVID GUETTA ft KELLY ROWLAND

40. *LoveSong* 2011 - ADELE

Total maximum Score: 43 POINTS   Your Score:

If you scored 35-43 - FANTASTIC - but you may need a bit more Bible and a bit less music?
If you scored 25-35 - GREAT JOB - but how about adding an audio Bible to your music collection?
If you scored 15-25 - ROOM FOR IMPROVEMENT - maybe a bit of background music during your Bible reading?
If you scored less than 15 - OH DEAR! Still, there's no condemnation in Christ Jesus - You just may need a bit more music and a little less Bible!

Appendix D: Acknowledgements

Through the first-time experience of writing and publishing a book, I have discovered some things that I wasn't expecting.
[These are probably common findings for most first-time authors.]

The first has been that when I started to write, I had no idea what the finished product would look like. What you read somehow 'evolved', and even now, I'm not quite sure how.

A second thing is that 'LoveSong' has taken far longer to review, edit and correct than to write.

But above all, I have realised there are many, many people over the years who have knowingly and unknowingly contributed to this book being written. My deep gratitude goes out to:

Ben Parker for the fantastic artwork and cover design.

The team at New Generation Publishing – who have helped me through each stage.

Mike Scott, whose lyrics inspire and lift me always. It is a privilege to use some in this book. In doing so, full acknowledgements to Sony Music/ATV Ltd, Chrysalis Records Ltd, and W14 Music.

The congregations, leaders and friends I have encountered in the stages of my journey, from the following Churches: Grantham Baptist Church, Dereham Baptist Church, Breckland Christian Fellowship Swaffham, and Living Well Church Rotorua. You all have taught me different parts of the Song.

Not Forgetting to raise a glass of love and thanks to Codgers Everywhere!

More recently, to the congregation, leaders, Prime-timers and friends at Ridgeway Church Chingford, who supported Kirsten and myself during our 13 years as leaders. We came to teach you the song, and left having learnt more verses to it.

To Gary Ellis who back in 1998, told me I would one day write a book and to Valentin Yombo, who reminded me 20 years later that I needed to.

To Susi Barber. Thank you for your countless hours editing and for your massive encouragement, and to you and John for your prayers and friendship for K & I through the chapters of our life.

To the Parker Clan, taking a Polaroid Picture right now (nod to Frank Turner) Mum, Dad, Ben, Dom, K and Padders – everything really is OK. Thank You.

To my New Zealand Family – the song is for you too!

To Kirsten, my beautiful, wonderful wife who is my harshest critic (the pages of the book have just about stopped bleeding but are way better for it) and my best friend who God has given me to learn and sing the song with together through life. I am thankful beyond words.

Father, Son, Spirit – The LoveSong. Forever. Thank you

Lightning Source UK Ltd.
Milton Keynes UK
UKHW011244221021
392644UK00002B/57